The Profit Hunter

BEATING THE BULLS, TAMING THE BEARS, AND SLAUGHTERING THE PIGS

Neil DeFalco

Oakshire Financial

WILEY

John Wiley & Sons, Inc.

Published by John Wiley & Sons, Inc., Hoboken, New Jersey.

Published simultaneously in Canada.

For general information on our other products and services or for technical support, please contact our Customer Care Department within the United States at (800) 762-2974, outside the United States at (317) 572-3993 or fax (317) 572-4002.

Wiley also publishes its books in a variety of electronic formats. Some content that appears in print may not be available in electronic books. For more information about Wiley products, visit our web site at www.wiley.com.

Library of Congress Cataloging-in-Publication Data:

DeFalco, Neil.
    The profit hunter : beating the bulls, taming the bears, and slaughtering the pigs / Neil DeFalco.
      p. cm.
    Includes index.
    ISBN 978-0-470-53874-6 (cloth)
    1. Investments. 2. Speculation. I. Title.
    HG4521.D478 2010
    332.6–dc22

                                                            2009045967

Printed in the United States of America

10 9 8 7 6 5 4 3 2 1

I dedicate this book to the citizens of the United States of America. Notably, all of my friends and family—without which, I would be just another vapid capitalist. All of you have keep me grounded in reality—which some would say is highly important...

Contents

v

Preface

We have witnessed a lot these past couple years with the Credit Crisis, housing collapse, the misappropriation of the TARP funds, the national debt at about 90 percent of GPD—and I think it's safe to say at this point that you cannot rely on the government to help secure your retirement or financial future.

The Profit Hunter will help you take the right steps toward increasing your net worth, and by doing so, allow you to stabilize your finances and help you live the life that you have always wanted to. Using the investing techniques and philosophies in this book, you can finally build up some capital and break free of the monotonous, day-to-day grind that so many people suffer through their whole life.

The reality is that we live in a world dominated by money—and without it, you really can't do anything. It doesn't matter if your dream is to feed starving children abroad or to buy your own private island.

I think most people will agree that if you were to have a couple million dollars in the bank, you could go to a place like Africa—build a school, construct a decent housing development, or help put together a functioning sewage system. With some money, you can actually *create* the programs that make a difference.

I'm well aware that this is a somewhat ugly reality, but it's a reality none the less. I have nothing against idealism—it helps push us forward—but without money, idealism has a hard time materializing. The Peace Corps, Save the Children, and every other charity you know of—simply cannot operate without proper funding. So the big question becomes: How do you rack up the dollars?

The first option is to work—but unless you have a Harvard MBA—you're probably going to be making just enough to get by for most of your life. In your earlier years, you'll rack up debt and spend the rest of your adult life trying to pay it off. The second option is to steal it—but we all know that this is futile and will only land you in jail. However, the third option is to invest and make solid returns—and that's where *The Profit Hunter* comes into play.

In this book, I provide a variety of ways to make money in bull markets, bear markets, and pig markets using derivative securities and hedging strategies. These are strategies that people have been using for decades to increase their net worth and stabilize their future. Take the more popular Horatio Alger, rags-to-riches stories on Wall Street—Timothy Sykes, for example. He took $12,000 in bar mitzvah money and turned it into $2 million in the early 2000s by using strategies similar to those that are discussed in this book. He parlayed his earnings into a hedge fund and is now living his dream.

Then, there is John William Henry—the current owner of the Boston Red Sox. He made his fortune by hedge trading corn and soybean futures. Eventually, John started his own commodities management firm and is now worth over $800 million.

These guys are perfect modern examples of the American Dream coming to fruition. And the best part about it is that they used the stock market to make it happen. If these guys can do it, then so can you.

The American Dream is no fallacy; it's as real as parades and parking tickets. Take my story, for example: The son of an Irish immigrant, I grew up in a modest household, attended public high school, and went to a state college. I didn't have Ivy League parents or a trust fund to lean on. All I had was my pride, some audacity, and a little bit of nerve.

And that is what capitalism is all about—the old dinosaurs dying and the young and hungry coming up with new ideas, better business models, and more efficient operations, all in an effort to make some money and stake their claims.

Whatever your dreams and aspirations are, *you have to go for it.* Put the wheels in motion *now*, before it is too late. Start making and saving capital by using the best moneymaking machine in the world: the American stock market.

Acknowledgments

A special thanks to Shannon Roxborough, Roland Lim Heng Wee, Nicholas Jones, and Damon Wright for helping me with the research process. Also, a special thanks to Steve Oakes—you're a good guy and great business partner—thanks for keeping a guy level headed.

CHAPTER 1

The Wall Street Revolution: Out with the Old and In with the New

First things first: In order to embark on this wealth-building journey, you will need to adjust your current investment mindset. You will come to realize that the traditional retail brokerage industry is dying and that the only way to really make any money is to manage your own investments.

This chapter will establish why the traditional brokerage industry is a failed prospect for the common investor and how the industry as a whole is becoming a thing of the past. From an inside perspective, I will show you how the average investor can use independent investment research coupled with discount online brokerage accounts to significantly cut down on overall investment costs while still receiving the "advantageous" individual investment advice touted by the traditional brokerage industry. Given the current times, I will also shed light on the credit crisis, the Troubled Asset Relief Program (TARP), and how corruption on Wall Street caused one of the worst market collapses in modern history.

This book provides investment strategies and techniques for profiting in bull, bear, and pig markets for the small- to medium-sized investor using derivative securities and hedging techniques.

The Profit Hunter is for the average investor to use as a tool to gather wealth and break free of the daily grind that plagues so many people's lives. If you already have millions of dollars, then I applaud you, you're already chopping the moon.

The Downfall of the Traditional, Full-Service Brokerage Industry

In just 10 short years, we have witnessed two of the largest bull-bear swings in American stock market history—an environment some would say has become more eccentric than Patrick Bateman and his Chiru bedsheets in the movie *American Psycho*.

Fortunes have been gained and lost—and in some situations, investors have lost absolutely everything. As the old saying goes, "Fool me once, shame on you; fool me twice, shame on me." That was a sentiment that rang deep for a lot of investors after the tech bubble burst in the early 2000s and is now once again a feeling that a lot of investors are burdened with since the housing bubble burst in 2008.

The so-called "Jewels of Wall Street" have failed them. The traditional, brick-and-mortar, button-down brokerage firms and the investment advisors that worked for them—who promised customized individual investment advice, complete risk diversification, and service next to none—have lost most, if not all, of their clients' money.

As it turns out, the old money management sales pitch of the well-dressed, suspender-wearing investment advisor was complete malarkey. When it came down to it, the fancy offices and the promises of risk mitigation and best-interest practices were just the lubricant to squeeze you through the door. In the end, you lost money—and a lot of it, too.

It's a grim, slaughterhouse reality that many investors were forced to realize during the first decade of the twenty-first century.

What Happened, and Why?

When I refer to the traditional brokerage industry, I am talking about Wall Street broker/dealers, more commonly known as investment banks. I use the terms broker/dealers and investment banks interchangeably throughout this chapter.

What is a broker/dealer? A broker/dealer is a company that trades securities for its own account (dealer) and on behalf of its customers (broker). The following is a list of the largest broker/dealers acting in the United States:

- Bank of America Securities, LLC
- Merrill Lynch
- Barclays Capital, Inc.

- Cantor Fitzgerald & Co.
- Citigroup Global Markets, Inc.
- Credit Suisse Securities, LLC
- Deutsche Bank Securities, Inc.
- Goldman, Sachs & Co.
- HSBC Securities, Inc.
- J.P. Morgan Securities, Inc.
- Morgan Stanley & Co., Inc.
- Smith Barney
- RBC Securities, Inc.
- UBS Securities, LLC

These companies control trillions of dollars in assets and are home to the vast majority of American investment brokerage accounts. Millions upon millions of average investors trade stocks, bonds, and a wide variety of other securities through these firms on a daily basis.

Now, answer this: Do you know what the difference is between a broker/dealer and a registered investment advisor?

Well, studies suggest that as many as 75 percent of Americans do not. And this is one of the major problems with the traditional brokerage industry today.

People in the financial business currently have the autonomy to use whatever moniker they see fit—be it "investment advisor," "financial advisor," "financial planner," "wealth management advisor," or "financial consultant," just to name some of the more popular ones. And the problem is that none of these terms adequately describe what these people are paid to do.

Back in the days prior to 2000, the line between the two was very clear. "Broker/dealer representatives" or "stockbrokers" were salespeople. They would buy and sell securities for clients and provide advice on that single transaction. They did not get paid for advice; they got paid on sales. And like many salespeople, they only came around when they had something to sell and did not make a living by providing service on the products that they sold.

On the other hand, registered investment advisors were fee based and managed clients' assets in a fiduciary role. In theory, this fee-based compensation encouraged the investment advisor to provide *objective* investment advice to their clients and to always act in their clients' best interests (fiduciary duty).

However, since the Securities and Exchange Commission (SEC) began pushing the "Merrill Lynch Law" in 1999—which gave broker/dealers the ability to offer clients fee-based accounts and basically the ability to act as false fiduciaries—the difference between the two has become muddled.

Today, broker/dealer representatives or stockbrokers working for many of the large broker/dealers like Merrill Lynch, UBS, and Morgan Stanley continue to call themselves "financial advisors" or "wealth management consultants," pretending to act in their clients' best interests, when this really is not the case.

Broker/dealers are held to what is called a "suitability standard," meaning they only have to do what is *suitable* for the client. A fee-only investment advisor is held to a "fiduciary standard," meaning they must do what is *best* for their client. This can sometimes be a confusing concept, so allow me to illustrate.

Suppose that a large cap growth mutual fund is a suitable investment for a certain client. As any investor knows, there are tons of equity large cap growth mutual funds out there to choose from, so for the sake of simplicity, say that the advisor is looking at two different funds. One fund has an expense ratio of 1.0 percent and pays a 0.50 percent commission to the salesperson. The other fund has an expense ratio of 0.90 percent and pays no commission to the salesperson.

As long as both funds are "suitable" for the client, a broker/dealer representative or stockbroker is allowed to recommend the fund that pays the higher sales commission. On the other hand, a registered investment advisor is obligated to recommend the fund with the lower expense ratio, because it provides the client with the possibility of better returns (not as many overhead costs eating into profits) at the end of the year.

It is clear to see the conflict of interest there. And I think it is obvious that there need be laws in place that require a company to make a definite distinction as to whether its account representatives are broker/dealer representatives or registered investment advisors.

There have been attempts to make distinctions between the two over the last few years. Take the overturning of the aforementioned "Merrill Lynch Law" in 2007 by the U.S. Court of Appeals—a step in the right direction in forcing broker/dealers to either register as investment advisors or to do away with fee-based accounts altogether. There was also talk of making it mandatory for broker/

dealers to have disclosure statements on all new account forms, basically explaining that their interests conflict with the clients' best interests.

However, trying to reform an industry where a few very powerful organizations rule the roost in a country where big business and government sleep in the same bedroom will be slow, ugly, and quite possibly futile. The broker/dealers that I previously listed control over $10 trillion in assets and employ over one million people; they have powerful connections in Washington, DC, and passing legislation that will hurt their best interests will be difficult.

Here I am, writing this book in the fall of 2009, two years after the "Merrill Lynch Law" was overturned, and when I do a Web search for "Merrill Lynch," the first thing I see is their web site, which reads, "Merrill Lynch—Financial Management and Advisory."

To the average investor, this still gives the impression of best-interest practices, which is not the case. This needs to be understood by the investing public.

The "Merrill Lynch Law" is not totally to blame for this whole conflict-of-interest mess. A lot of it goes back to the 1990s merger madness between Wall Street investment banks and independent investment brokerage firms. Some examples are the merger of UBS and PaineWebber in 2000, the merger of Morgan Stanley and Dean Witter in 1997, and the merger of Solomon Brothers and Smith Barney/Travelers/Citigroup in 1998.

These companies were following what appeared to be a brilliant business model held by Merrill Lynch, who had both an investment banking division and a huge brokerage force with thousands of individual investor accounts. This created a synergy that gave Merrill Lynch the ability to directly place securities that its investment banking division underwrote.

Before the mergers of the 1990s, investment banks like Morgan Stanley and Solomon Brothers had to rely on groups of independent brokers like Dean Witter and Smith Barney to buy and distribute underwritten securities like initial public offerings (IPOs), mutual funds, and other structured products. It seemed only logical to combine the two segments of the industry. In theory, this would allow for large cuts in variable overhead costs, thus streamlining operations and increasing efficiency.

However, what everyone seemed to ignore was the huge conflict of interest that would arise with the acquired brokerage firms and all the investment advisors handling individual investor accounts. By gaining the ability to place underwritten securities and IPOs through an in-house brokerage network, a firm basically subverts the advisor's fiduciary responsibility to his or her clients.

Investment banks profit by raising money for companies and governments through issuing and selling securities and then taking a commission on the total amount. The more commonly known security produced by investment banks is the initial public offering of stock, or IPO. Investment banks are also responsible for the dreaded collateralized debt obligations (CDOs), the very product that caused the housing bubble—which I will get into later.

Using the basic law of supply and demand, it's easy to understand that the more demand there is for a product, the higher the price of the product will be and the more money the investment bank will make on the commission. This gives incentive for the investment banking side of the firm to push the investment advisory side of the firm to sell newly underwritten securities to individual investors and offer a monetary bonus to do so.

The mergers of the 1990s proved fruitful for the investment banks. With the newly acquired brokerage force and all of its client capital, the investment banking division could now somewhat control the demand for newly underwritten securities, thus creating the public perception that the security was highly desired, therefore raising the price of the product and creating more commission for the investment bank.

We can be sure of one thing: The investment banking divisions of the broker/dealers that I previously listed don't give a damn about your money or the performance of your account.

And that is why there were registered investment advisors in the first place—to protect average investors from being taken advantage of. But when the investment banks bought up a large majority of independent brokerage firms in the 1990s, there was this sudden influx of advisors that no longer had fiduciary responsibility, and this was easily exploited with the SEC's push of the "Merrill Lynch Law" in 1999.

In the Mind of the "Investment Advisor"

As I stated earlier, investment banks (broker/dealers) like Morgan Stanley and Merrill Lynch want their stockbrokers to give the appearance of having a fiduciary responsibility to their clients, so they offer fee-based accounts and refer to their stockbrokers as "investment advisors" or "wealth management consultants" or "financial advisors"—but don't be fooled.

What you need to realize is that even though you have a fee-based account and your so-called "investment advisor" says they are not compensated directly for making trades on your behalf, they do receive compensation via product placement fees.

As a former financial advisor, I can tell you that on a daily basis, either third-party investment organizations or the in-house investment bankers would take all of the financial advisors out to lunch and pitch mutual funds and structured products to us, offering monetary bonuses for placing clients in their products—be it mutual funds, bonds, stocks, managed futures, or structured products such as collateralized debt obligations.

Basically, as the client, you are losing money either way—fee-based account or not. I can assure you that your investment advisor is going to put your money in the funds that provide him or her the most commission—regardless of the quality. I couldn't tell you the number of free lobster lunches I sat through, listening to some salesperson trying to convince me to put my clients' money in whatever the hot product of the week was.

Take the following quote off Morgan Stanley Smith Barney's web site. This quote says it all, but I can assure you that most people have never seen it:

> Morgan Stanley Smith Barney and its affiliates may earn compensation in other, more indirect ways with regard to certain of the products you purchase or services you receive. For example, Morgan Stanley Smith Barney may earn compensation in connection with the provision of investment banking, prime brokerage, institutional brokerage or placement agent services, as well as stock loan or other lending, money-management or trading-desk activities. Certain investment vehicles may include securities of Morgan Stanley Smith Barney's parent or other affiliates and companies in which Morgan Stanley or its affiliates make a market or in which Morgan Stanley Smith Barney or the officers or employees of Morgan Stanley Smith Barney or Morgan Stanley Smith Barney's affiliates own securities.
>
> *September 2009,*
> *www.morganstanleyindividual.com/ourcommitment/*
> *compensation.asp*

There are two things on a financial advisor's mind at all times: acquiring more assets to manage and placing those assets into investment vehicles that make the most commission.

The typical financial advisor is constantly entangled with the moral dilemma of either doing what is right for the client or making as much money as possible. And the truth of the matter is that most of them fall into the latter category.

Too many people believe that their financial advisor has their best interest at heart, but let me assure you that this is not the case; they are the sharks, and their clients are the minnows.

And until there are laws in place that require firms to distinctly distinguish between stockbrokers and financial advisors—and to verbally tell potential clients about conflicts of interest in compensation—then investors will never know if their financial advisor is really acting in their best interests or if he or she is just a glorified salesperson.

You are probably thinking to yourself that it doesn't make much sense for a financial advisor to place your assets into securities that aren't really suited for you in the first place—because if the end game is to acquire more assets, then why would they risk losing your money?

That would make the most sense. However, it's a money game, and the large accounts pay more than the small accounts. So, if you are a small account—say, under $50,000—with no additional capital to invest, then you aren't making your financial advisor any real money in terms of 1 to 2 percent management fees, eventually leading them to resort to exploiting the sales/placement commission side of their compensation.

The first time I was exposed to this reality was when I was working as an intern for a senior vice president of investments (common title for a high-earning investment advisor) in college. I remember the overall philosophy among the financial advisors was to close as many accounts as possible, no matter the size of the account, because every advisor assumed that all clients lied to them about their true net worth.

Once they closed a client, the advisor would allocate the new assets into extremely conservative investments and products that would provide a return of a couple points above interest rates— usually a complex arrangement of bonds with some conservative equity funds.

The advisor would then sit on the account for exactly six months to prove to the new client that they were worth their salt and could provide a respectable return. Then, the hard sell would ensue for up to a month in an effort to squeeze out every liquid penny possible from the new client.

At the end of the first six or seven months, if the client's account didn't total more than $100,000, they would be put into the burn file. This file was basically forgotten, until there was some sort of fund or structured product that either the investment banking side of the firm recently developed or an outside institution was offering that would pay an extra bonus on every sale or placement.

Then, all hell would break loose, and it became a competition among the financial advisors to see who could sell the most. You would hear everything from "This is the next Google," to "If you don't get into this IPO, you are going to be crying in the corner come six months when it more than triples."

Eventually, someone would come out on top. It was a great time for everyone but the client, who didn't know what was really going on.

As you can see, the investment banking/brokerage mergers of the 1990s along with the "Merrill Lynch Law" have created a serious conflict of interest in the traditional investment banking/brokerage community. These conflicts have affected millions of investors all over the world. People thought that they were in the hands of advisors who had their best interests in mind, but they truly didn't and still don't.

However, today, investors have options that they never had before—the Internet, online investment brokers, and independent investment research. The common investor no longer needs to be subjected to the egregious behavior of the traditional brokerage firms or to deal with investment advisors that throw your money into whatever pays them the largest placement fee, regardless of quality.

There are two lessons to be learned here. One: If you have less than $100,000 invested in the stock market with a traditional full-service brokerage firm like UBS, Morgan Stanley, and so on, get out and open an online brokerage account. Your financial advisor will try to sell you on the benefits of having independent investment advice—but with the burgeoning independent investment research industry (which I will cover in a moment), you can get all the investment advice that you need.

Two: If you have too much money to manage yourself and need a full-service broker, make sure to find an advisor that is not associated with a broker/dealer or investment bank. Ask them if they receive placement commissions from third-party companies. If they say no, get it in writing. Do your own research or purchase independent investment research so that you can be the navigator of your financial future and keep abreast of what's going on in the investing world. And most of all, if your advisor calls you to tell you about a new, awesome, unknown investment opportunity that is going to make you a millionaire overnight, don't buy it—because chances are that he or she is just trying to make a little money on the side, regardless of how it affects you.

The Average Investor's Savior: The Online Brokerage Industry

With the advent of the Internet and electronic communications networks (ECNs) in the mid- to late-1990s, the world of investing has begun a change that will last well into the future. The Internet has opened the flood gates to millions of "mini-investors" that once couldn't get the time of day at a traditional brokerage firm. These mini-investors are now trading daily via online brokerages and creating a sort of safe haven for the common investor—a place where they can actively trade without the burden of the high fees and the constant harassment of a stockbroker trying to sell them the next hot product.

Since the tech bubble burst in the early 2000s, an exodus has begun. Where the once all-powerful brick-and-mortar broker/dealers like Merrill Lynch and Morgan Stanley ruled the walk, Wall Street is now seeing droves of investors move their accounts into the world of online brokerage firms, such as Fidelity, Interactive Brokers, and Scottrade.

These newfound online brokerage firms created competition and offered the same trading services as the traditional full-service brokers but at a fraction of the cost. It truly was a godsend for your average investor with less than $50,000 in liquid investment capital. People realized that being raped on commissions while being wooed by disingenuous fiduciaries was a reality no longer.

Capitalism breeds change; it drives technology and innovation, and it keeps competition constantly evolving. If the old and inefficient can't keep up, then they are pushed out. And this is the perfect example—the traditional, full-service, button-down, dinosaur broker/dealers losing a significant share of the investment brokerage market to more efficient, faster, and cheaper online brokerage firms. The online brokerage industry has been flourishing since the late-1990s, and it's still growing year after year—even through the credit crisis and stock market crash of 2008.

During 2008, TD Ameritrade saw net new asset growth of over 60 percent, while companies like TradeKing saw 40 to 50 percent growth in new brokerage accounts. Online brokerage firms were growing, while their traditional counterparts like Bear Stearns and Lehman Brothers were going bankrupt.

The investing public is trading, growing, and managing their assets online. Now, it isn't like the Morgans and Merrills of the industry couldn't adapt—they just chose not to. It is a classic case of the old and tired lacking motivation—and in today's economy, that is a recipe for disaster.

This resistance to change, coupled with the tech bubble blow out in 2001, created a perfect environment for the online brokerage industry to thrive. Recently burned investors were looking for change. They realized that nobody could manage their money better than they could, and online brokerages offered these investors a refuge.

With the baby boomer retirement cycle off and running since January 2008, 76 million Americans born between 1946 and 1960 will start to gain access to retirement plans such as 401ks, individual retirement accounts (IRAs), and pensions. Money will start to flow from institutional funds into personal investment accounts. These newly retired individuals will have more time to direct toward their investments.

Like I said before, "Fool me once, shame on you; fool me twice, shame on me." These baby boomers control the majority of wealth in this country. They are the ones who have been burned by the tech and housing bubbles, and if anyone is going to want to manage their own money, it is going to be the baby boomers.

Of course, there is the fact that most online brokerage firms do not provide clients with investment advice. And let's be honest: Most people don't have time to spend scouting stocks and learning all the ins and outs of financial analysis. But there is no need to worry. With the up-and-coming independent investment research industry (which I'll go over shortly)—composed of companies like Oakshire Financial, Angel Publishing, Motley Fool, and Schaeffers Investment Research—the online brokerage investors can get all the investment advice they need, from highly experienced financial analysts, without all the attached Wall Street corruption of the traditional brokerage firms like UBS and Merrill Lynch.

We are witnessing a whole new animal altogether. We are entering a period where bull markets are quicker to strike, and the bear markets are more severe; the capital market mood swings are becoming more and more rapid as technology delivers information faster and faster. The individual investor has the ability to trade, and trade actively, with online brokerage accounts and is becoming a dominant force in the market.

It is an interesting time, to say the least. Technology is taking over, and efficiency is the name of the game. If you have an online trading account, that's great. If you don't, it is time to switch. The train is pulling out of the station, and you don't want to be left behind. Now, all you need is some alternative, independent investment advice, and you'll be on the right track.

Independent Investment Research and Analysis: Wall Street's Biggest Threat

Since the advent of the Internet and the birth of the online brokerage industry, the traditional brokerage industry has sold investors on one thing—individual investment advice. The argument has been that while online brokerage firms like Scottrade, E*Trade, and Interactive Brokers do provide investors with a much more affordable means to invest, they do not provide their clients with customized, personal investment advice. And since most investors do not have a formal education in finance or years of experience, they really don't know what they are doing and will lose money from making bad investment decisions.

These statements are true, for the most part. The majority of investors do not have an education in finance or years of experience trading. But with the blossoming independent investment research industry and books like this one, the average investor can receive all the investment advice they need, without paying exorbitant fees to financial advisors.

The independent investment research and analysis industry came into its own during the mid-1990s, around the same time that the online brokerage industry started to flourish. While independent investment research has been around since the days when ratings agencies like Moody's were founded, it really didn't become a force to be reckoned with until the advent of the Internet.

The Internet gave independent analysts the ability to publish and deliver investment research at a fraction of the cost. It broke down the barrier of entry.

Before the Internet and e-mail, information was printed and mailed. The overhead costs were astronomical and were passed on to the consumer in the form of extremely expensive subscription fees. Qualified investment research was often too expensive for the common investor.

With e-mail and web sites, the investment research industry is seeing an unprecedented level of competition. Research has to be top-notch, and the analysts are more qualified than ever. Investors have plenty of options to choose from, and since independent investment research newsletters are much more reasonably priced today, investors can pick and choose without breaking the bank.

The online brokerage industry and independent investment research go together like coffee and the pot—one provides the sustenance, and the other provides the mode of delivery. Now, there are many different kinds of coffee and several types of pots; some pots cost less than others, and some brands of coffee taste better. However, they all satisfy your caffeine craving in the end.

It all comes down to preference—and choosing which independent investment research newsletters to subscribe to is no different. The following is a list of the more prominent research firms out there today:

- Oakshire Financial
- Angel Publishing
- Schaeffer's Investment Research
- Investor Place Media
- Motley Fool
- Horizon Publishing
- The Oxford Club

These companies offer a wide variety of investment research and analysis newsletters—whether on stocks, bonds, mutual funds, futures, the foreign exchange (FOREX) market, options, or real estate. You can find everything you need from these companies.

For example, my company, Oakshire Financial, concentrates on stock option and income investing. Angel Publishing, on the other hand, is a front-runner in alternative energy investing. No matter what your tastes are, you can find them. You just have to spend some time and look at what each firm has to offer.

What makes the independent investment research industry so beneficial and unique is that it's not plagued and entangled in the bureaucracy of Wall Street. Unlike the major ratings agencies, which are paid by companies to analyze their stock, the independent research firms have no incentive other than to sell more subscriptions to their newsletters—and the only way to do that is to provide subscribers with sound analysis that makes them money. These firms have the ability to keep bias aside and to produce truly uninfluenced investment research and analysis.

Companies like Oakshire Financial are part of a growing collective of outsiders in a world where being on the inside is coveted. As we have seen, the old boys' club on Wall Street has done more harm than good over the last decade. It is time for an adjustment, and the independent investment research community is leading the charge for change on the frontier that is the American financial markets.

With all of that said, I hope that you will take a more active role in your investing. After reading this book, if you do not leave your financial advisor immediately for an online brokerage account, then at least subscribe to some independent research, use the techniques outlined later in this book, and take charge of your financial future— because the simple fact of the matter is that nobody will look out for your money better than you, and anyone who says they can is just trying to dip into your nest egg for their own benefit.

Take a look at the recent recession—even the U.S. government would rather give your money to the very companies that caused you to lose half your net worth in the stock market crash of 2008 rather than properly fix the conflict of interest and corruption on Wall Street between securities ratings agencies and investment banks.

The crash was bad, yes; but shouldn't the punishment for bad business decisions be failure of business? It certainly shouldn't be a trip to Vegas on the taxpayer's dime. I know that letting certain companies fail would have caused a more severe economic meltdown. But when should we draw the line? The U.S. government bailed out AIG to the tune of 80 percent of its equity. That sounds like nationalization to me. So, will profits from AIG going forward be divided up and sent to every American taxpayer? Do I get to vote at the shareholders' meetings now? If AIG fails and they liquidate all of its assets, will I have a say in what happens to that money?

Unfortunately, the answer to all of those questions is no. I could write a whole other book on the problems of the government bailing out business, but for now I'll just touch on how we got to the bailouts in the first place.

The Corruption That Caused the Credit Crisis

Given the recent recession, housing bubble, and stock market meltdown, I wouldn't be doing anyone any justice if I didn't go over the credit crisis, how it happened, and what caused it.

Let's start from the very beginning.

In 1938, the U.S. government created an agency called the Federal National Mortgage Association, or Fannie Mae, with the sole purpose of making homeownership available to low-income housing residents by purchasing the loans from the originators (mainly savings and loan associations). This freed up capital for the originators, thus allowing them to make more loans and effectively guaranteeing the value of the mortgages by the U.S. government.

Fannie Mae was the only one in its space until 1968, when the government split the agency into two parts—a private corporation and a publicly financed institution. The private, shareholder-owned corporation still utilized the moniker Fannie Mae and continued to purchase mortgages, but it did so without the government guarantee of repayment. The publicly financed institution was named the Government National Mortgage Association, or Ginny Mae, and explicitly guaranteed the repayment of principle and interest on mortgages made to government employees and veterans.

Then, in 1970, using the Emergency Home Finance Act of 1970, the government created a new, public, shareholder-owned company called the Federal Home Loan Corporation, or Freddie Mac, to compete with the newly public Fannie Mae and to facilitate a more liquid and efficient secondary mortgage market.

All three of these firms package or pool mortgages by risk and sell them on the open market to investors in the form of mortgage-backed securities (MBS). Their primary form of income is charging (Freddie and Fannie) or offering (Ginny) a guarantee fee for repayment. Freddie Mac and Fannie Mae, although public companies, are heavily subsidized by the government; however, their MBS are not guaranteed by the government. Only Ginny Mae MBS are fully guaranteed by the government.

For 30 years, these organizations ruled the MBS market. They had strict rules on what kind of mortgages they would purchase (often only good-credit applicants and above with enough capital to make a significant down payment) and engaged in almost oligopolistic behavior—which they could do, since they were the only firms offering to mitigate the risk for mortgage loan originators.

Freddie and Fannie were basically the leaders of the mortgage market until the early 2000s, when both firms became entangled in accounting scandals and subsequently lost their dominance of the mortgage industry. This allowed the mortgage lenders to change the rules—once so heavily imposed by Freddie and Fannie—and all they needed was someone with large amounts of capital who would be more willing to bend the rules. They found that someone on Wall Street. Wall Street investment banks saw this as the opportunity of a lifetime; with a cash-heavy world economy, U.S. interest rates at all-time lows, Chinese and Indian economies booming, and oil dollars flooding into the Middle East, there was a high demand for safe, steady, and stable paying investments—something that MBS were extremely well known for.

To feed the growing demand, Wall Street pushed mortgage originators to generate more loans. And in order to do this, the mortgage originators started underwriting a lot of loans to the subprime borrower. It started out with borrowers who had good credit but couldn't afford a down payment and ended up with borrowers who had bad credit and couldn't afford a down payment. It got to the point where mortgage originators were employing a stated income policy, which didn't require borrowers to prove how much money they made.

You are probably asking yourself: Didn't the investment banks on Wall Street see how bad this was? That the risk was going to be too high? The answer is simply that if one firm didn't do it, then another firm would. It was like the Wild West. There were all of these mortgage originators turning out hundreds of millions of dollars in loans each month and this huge demand from around the world for MBS—Wall Street investment banks just acted as the middle man.

It was at this time, in the early 2000s, that the adjustable rate mortgage (ARM) became terribly popular—increasing in a percentage relative to 30-year fixed mortgages from 2 percent in 1998 to over 27 percent in 2004. These ARMs would often come with a "teaser" fixed interest rate payment in the beginning—the most popular being the Hybrid 3/1 ARM. This ARM would have a very low monthly payment for the first three years of the mortgage and then one year of payments that would be much higher than normal interest rates—thus raising the monthly mortgage payment significantly.

These ARMs were a perfect product for the mortgage originators; once shunned by Freddie and Fannie, they were now loved by Wall Street. The ARM would allow mortgage originators to underwrite loans based on the borrower's initial, ultralow "teaser" mortgage payments, which were obviously below the fully amortizing payment level—thus allowing the borrower to take on much more debt and receive a much higher mortgage than would otherwise be possible.

As you can see from the chart in Figure 1.1, during 2004, 2005, and 2006, interest rates, off of which the initial fixed part of the

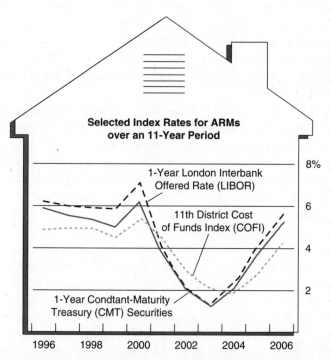

Figure 1.1   Selected Index Rates for ARMs over an 11-Year Period

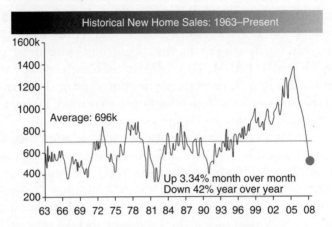

Figure 1.2   Historical New Home Sales: 1963–Present
Source: http://seekingalpha.com/article/79103-historical-new-home-sales-chart

classic 3/1 ARM was based, were extraordinarily low. This also happens to be when mortgage sales were the absolute highest. (See Figure 1.2.) Therefore, this created the perfect market for the subprime mortgage; over 20 percent of all mortgage originations were of the subprime persuasion between the years 2004 and 2006. This was up substantially from the time period between 1996 and 2004, when subprime mortgages accounted for only 9 percent of total originations.

It is very easy to see the logic here. The mortgage originators would sell these loans to subprime borrowers with the assumption that after the three years of low fixed payments, the borrower would just refinance into another 3/1 ARM—and the cycle would continue. The fatal flaw in this equation is that interest rates would have to remain low, housing prices would have to continue to rise, and the subprime borrower would have to improve their credit score. None of these things happened.

At the time, money was flowing like water, and consumer spending was steadily rising each and every quarter—fueling an economic boom based on fictitious capital. American consumers were leveraged to the hilt.

And as you can see from the chart in Figure 1.2, the bottom fell out in late 2006/early 2007. With interest rates on the rise, borrowers with ARMs that originated in 2003 and 2004 started to see their monthly mortgage payments increase drastically—and being fully

Figure 1.3   Mortgage Defaults, 1979–2009
Source: http://interestrateroundup.blogspot.com/2009/05/mba-q1-delinquency-and-foreclosure.html

leveraged, these borrowers saw themselves in a situation where they could not afford their bills, and mortgage defaults started to rise. (See Figure 1.3.) This was the beginning of what we now call the credit crisis.

So, if investment banks on Wall Street were securitizing these ugly mortgages, who was buying them? Why would anyone buy such garbage?

Well, during the peak of the housing boom, investment banks on Wall Street started to push a more complex product called a collateralized debt obligation, or CDO. A CDO is simply a bundle of fixed-income securities—like mortgage-backed securities—put into one investment. The difference is that a CDO does not have to just be filled with mortgage-backed securities—it can be filled with anything.

So, at the peak of the housing bubble—when mortgages and loans were generally being given out to anybody with a social security number—there were a lot of high-risk investment vehicles for the investment banks to fill CDOs with and sell around the world and on Wall Street.

And as with all fixed-income securities like bonds, the higher the risk of the underlying entity, the higher the annual return is to the investor who invests in the security. So, on paper, these CDOs looked like a really good deal—a diversified array of loans bundled up into one investment that paid a fixed, market-beating, monthly return. It seemed too good to be true, and it turned out to be just that.

However, the average investor would never have known this, because most of these CDOs had been given the highest of ratings by agencies like Fitch, Moody's, and Standard and Poor's (S&P).

And there lies the issue—the conflict of interest: the securities ratings agencies. These agencies are supposed to rate securities and bonds based on risk. But the problem is that the agencies are paid by companies like Morgan Stanley and Credit Suisse to rate their structure products, stock, and debt.

When the investment banks issued new CDOs, they would present the ratings agencies with the particulars on the CDO and then a check for doing the rating themselves. Obviously, it turns out that most of the CDOs put out during the housing bubble were chock-full of terrible debt that wound up defaulting, yet most of these CDOs were rated AAA, anyway.

Because these CDOs were given the highest ratings possible and were yielding returns much higher than the market average, everyone leveraged themselves to the hilt on these new "magic" investment vehicles.

Everyone bought as much as they could—and it turned into a state of reverse diversification. Banks, hedge funds, pension funds, and even foreign governments were buying these CDOs by the bulk. Who could blame them? They had the highest ratings, so they seemed safe and provided a great return on investment—basically for no risk whatsoever. And the worst part is that banks were lending money to hedge funds and other entities so that they could invest more money in CDOs. Everyone was exposed in some way, shape, or form.

Then, all of a sudden, housing prices started to tumble, and mortgage defaults rose, eventually rendering a large portion of these collateralized debt obligations worthless. Huge chunks of money disappeared, people stopped paying their bills, and the CDOs stopped paying premiums. The stock market collapsed in

October 2008, and then scores of banks around the United States collapsed.

People who worked for 50 years in steel mills and factories—the backbone of mid-twentieth-century America—lost their entire savings. People were rendered homeless. Grandparents had to go back to work at places like Wal-Mart and McDonald's for $7 an hour to help keep their heads above water. So much for the "Golden Years." It's truly a travesty.

And there is only one group to blame: *the securities ratings agencies*—Moody's, Fitch, and Standard & Poor's. It is their job to rate products and steer the investing public to what is a good investment and what isn't. You can't blame the investment banks for coming up with the CDO; their job description is to be money mongers, and they will do whatever necessary to make a buck.

The ratings agencies are supposed to be the balance. If they had rated these CDOs noninvestment grade to begin with, then demand for the CDOs would not have been so high, the investment banks wouldn't have pressured mortgage originators so hard for more loans, and this mess could have been much less severe, if not avoided completely.

There could be several causes for this gross misconduct. Maybe the investment banks bribed the ratings agencies for the highest ratings possible, or perhaps the ratings agencies didn't want to lose any business by rating the CDOs noninvestment grade. Whatever happened, it was terrible. Following is a list of reasons why you should not trust any rating that Moody's, Fitch, or Standard & Poor's puts out:

- Ratings agencies do not downgrade companies fast enough. Take Enron, for example: It remained rated at investment grade until four days before the company went bankrupt—despite the ratings agencies knowing months before that the company had significant problems.
- Ratings agencies have far too close of a relationship with the companies they perform ratings on. Rating agency reps meet constantly, in person, with the management of companies they rate and provide advice on actions the company should take to maintain certain ratings.
- Ratings agencies are paid by the companies that rate them—not investors. This creates a perfect situation for unscrupulous

behavior on both sides of the transaction—especially given their close relationship to begin with.

- With only three ratings agencies of any significance—Moody's, Fitch, and Standard & Poor's—you could say they are a sort of oligopoly. The barriers of entry into the industry are steep; this can be deduced from Moody's high profit on revenues— greater than 50 percent gross margin. Moody's is making a huge profit on the costs of goods sold. There is no competition to drive prices down, and these three companies can easily fix the costs of performing ratings. Not to mention that the Federal Reserve requires that public companies be rated by at least two of the three ratings agencies, so it isn't like a company really has a choice.

Basically, the housing bubble and credit crisis all boil down to this deep-seated conflict of interest between Wall Street securities ratings agencies and investment banks. It's a clear-cut problem that seemed to escape the public eye amid all the government interventions, business bailouts, and market rescue plans.

The only media coverage of this problem was on a special report CNBC aired called "The House of Cards." I remember watching the special and being completely stunned that there wasn't more outrage over this nasty conflict of interest on Wall Street. Nobody was talking about it—and all the while, the government was throwing taxpayers' money left and right, bailing out everyone and their mothers, when it was the ratings agencies that were at fault.

Just recently, I was listening to *Marketplace* on National Public Radio, and the host was talking about all the large profits Goldman Sachs and Morgan Stanley made on collateralized loan obligations (CLOs, the brother of the CDOs) during the second quarter of 2009—right after the market crashed and the CDO mess was uncovered. The guest on the show was going on and on about how these CLOs are just CDOs with a different flavor and how the ratings agencies are still rating these as good debt when they are really full of bad loans.

So, the host asks the guest why this conflict of interest is still going on, and the guest quoted President Obama, who said that it was too complex of a situation to deal with at the moment.

Right around the same time—June 2009—a report came out that President Obama spared the ratings agencies in his new financial regulatory reform plan. He basically told them to be more careful and to pay more attention when rating structured products like collateralized debt obligations.

Basically, the government is going to let the ratings agencies slide on by without punishment or regulation. And if this isn't bad enough, then there's the Troubled Asset Relief Program.

The TARP

I'm all about the government helping out the people and trying to prevent economic meltdowns. That, after all, is the government's job. But what happens when the government makes a mistake? When is a mistake too big to ignore?

These are questions that came up, at least in my mind, in late 2008/early 2009, when the government announced the Troubled Asset Relief Program, or TARP. This $700 billion taxpayer-sponsored program was supposed to be given to banks in order to relieve their subprime mortgage exposure and facilitate lending but was instead used for company gain and self-interest. AIG executives took lavish vacations; Bank of America bought Merrill Lynch; Wells Fargo bought Wachovia; PNC bought National City.

The government basically cut these banks checks with no sort of stipulations or guidelines as to how they were supposed to use the money. The government told the taxpayers that these billion dollar bailouts were going to help facilitate lending, easy the pressure on the banking system, stimulate the economy, create jobs, and prevent a banking collapse.

This is my last revision of this book—March 8th, 2010—and unemployment is still around 10% and so far this year 26 banks have failed—not to mention the 140 banks that went under in 2009.

From my perspective, it seems that the only institutions that have benefited are the largest ones with the most political ties to Washington.

Instead of bailing out the big guys, the government should have flooded the Small Business Administration with funding and eased the process of acquiring an SBA loan. The federal and state governments should have drastically reduced taxes on small business and given them incentives to hire and expand. Small business accounts for over 90 percent of all employer firms and employs more than half of this countries eligible workforce.

The government obviously made a huge mistake here. And the taxpayers need to step up and make sure the government knows that we aren't happy. There are too many back door deals and such between Wall Street and Washington. Obama ran on a ticket of complete transparency and reform. I remember his speeches about saving "Main Street" and fighting corruption on Wall Street—and it seems that no more than a month after he got into office, Wall Street was taken care of and main street was forgotten about.

As a small business owner—I can tell you that it is almost impossible to procure a SBA loan. My partner and I tried for months when we launched our investment research firm—and we never even got a response. The little guy got screwed here. And we should demand that the promises Obama made during his campaign run for president be brought to fruition...

The recent Tea Party movement is refreshing—highly unorganized—but at least its good to know that some people still care about what goes on in the government and are willing to take some sort of stand.

I do have to ask though—where is the youth's voice in all of this? The tea party seems to be mainly made up of the baby boomer generation—the generation of the 60's. Is the youth so caught up in the worlds of YouTube and Facebook that they've forgotten what this country was founded on? Or do they just not care? Because if that is the case, then the U.S. is headed for a bleak future.

I love and use technology just as much as the next guy, but I certainly don't walk around the grocery store, oblivious to everyone around me, yelling into my Bluetooth headset like a complete lunactic.

Instead of constantly escaping through technology, we need to use it to maximize efficiency—not only with business but with the government as well. There have been some recent attempts by the government to do this, with web sites such as www.recovery.gov. I applaud the effort, but it shouldn't stop here—every single taxpayer dollar that is spent in every level of the government—should be tracked. The fact that a website like www.recovery.gov can exist, shows us that it is possible to have absolute transparency in the government.

I personally believe in more states rights and a much smaller federal government, but if we are going to have such a large, powerful, and far reaching federal government—then the taxpayers should also be more directly involved in the decisions.

Perhaps each senator and house representative should have a cell phone application or some sort of electronic device that is given to the eligible taxpaying citizens of his/her district. Upon proposing or voting on any legislation, the respective senator or representative should have to send a synopsis through to the people for a public opinion on said legislation. The consensus of the constituents and the voting record of the senator/house representative should then be made public knowledge on a web site that meticulously tracks all local and federal government spending.

This kind of total transparency will lead to a much higher rate of efficiency in the government, misappropriations will be minimized, and the people can have more control over what goes on. Of course this isn't going to happen overnight and there would have to be a few checks a balances—but it isn't such a far-fetched idea—a government for the people, by the people.

Conclusion

I think I have made it clear that the average investor should be highly wary of Wall Street. They can't trust the traditional brokerage firms, and they certainly can't trust the securities ratings agencies. Common investors are going to have to rely on themselves. And with the help of independent investment research and the use of the online brokerage industry, the average investor has options that will keep him or her at arm's length from Wall Street's misbehavior.

Throughout the rest of this book, I am going to go over a variety of options investment strategies that can be used on equities, commodities, or even FOREX to profit in any market condition—be it a bull, bear, or pig (sideways) market.

Some of these strategies are complex, and some are rather simple; you may already be familiar with some of them. I know that trading in options can sometimes be confusing, which is why most people tend to shy away from it. However, there is no reason to be intimidated. This book will lay out everything you need to succeed and will serve as your guide to acquiring newfound wealth.

At the end of the book, I will also go over the ins and outs of the commodities, FOREX, and single stock futures markets. These are exciting markets with plenty of profit opportunities—especially using the techniques outlined in this book.

Use this book as a guide to setting yourself free. Gather some wealth, and go do what you have always wanted to do. Remember that life is too short to be stuck in some awful cubical, angry that Stan from accounting ate the last donut. Grab the bull by the balls and make a change.

And most of all, don't let Wall Street or the government fool you.

CHAPTER

2

Options Investing: The
Bare Essentials

In Chapter 1, I discussed the flaws on Wall Street—from the faulty fiduciaries to the corrupt ratings agencies. I stressed switching to an online brokerage firm and using independent investment research and analysis to steer your own investing ship.

While those things are crucial to know and understand, there are other basics that the average investor needs to know before they embark on the journey to wealth. Diversification is key. While you might be excited and want to put all of your money into trading the options techniques outlined in this book, *do not do that.*

If the tech and housing bubbles taught us anything, it's that putting all of your eggs in one basket is fiscal suicide. Never do this—no matter how excited or successful of a trader you become. Investing needs to be a methodical process, not an emotional one.

In this chapter, I will also go over some basics about options investing, as well as certain fundamental cues to look for when scouting a stock to execute an option play on and pointers on when to buy and when to sell.

The great value investor Ben Graham once said, "Investing is most successful when it is most business-like." And he couldn't have said it any better. Trading can be fun and exciting, but it is crucial to find a successful method and stick to it.

Remember—invest with your mind, not with your heart.

Diversification: The Cornerstone of Solid Investing

As I am sure you have heard many times, diversification is key. I don't think I can stress this enough. I did my first options trade when I was eighteen years old. I bought calls on Abercrombie and Fitch in anticipation of a breakout earnings announcement. I was working retail for the company part-time, and I knew that they were killing sales with the new Hollister division—but the market wasn't really catching on to it.

Their previous earnings announcement was a major surprise, and the stock subsequently popped. So, I took the couple hundred bucks that I had to my name and bought as many call options as I could. They were dirt cheap—something like 5 cents a contract—so I bought 40 contracts.

I was a novice and had just started getting into the stock market. I had read some information about stock options, but I didn't really know what I was doing. I placed the order on a Monday, and the earnings announcement was on that Thursday. Needless to say, I was glued to the computer screen. On Thursday morning, they announced the earnings, which beat expectations, and my call options were now in the money by 50 cents. I was ecstatic—my $200 grew into $2,000 in just four days!

I was terribly pleased with myself, to say the least. I told everyone at work about my newfound glory, and for the rest of the day, I just kept thinking about how the stock price was bound to go up more with such a killer earnings announcement. I was finally going to be able to buy that convertible I always wanted.

That night, I went out to a party and had a good time. I took off from school the next day and went skiing with a bunch of friends. As soon as I got home, I went to the computer to see if my options had appreciated. But to my utter surprise, there was no money in my account. At first, I panicked—I thought I had been robbed. I called customer service and started yelling into the phone, only to find out that my option contracts expired that Friday. I had overlooked the fact that options expire on the third Friday of the month, and I felt like a complete moron. My ignorance was the thief.

I was depressed for days, but eventually I got over it. The moral of the story is to never put all your money into one investment—or sector, for that matter. Given, my loss was sheer stupidity—and not

Figure 2.1 Gold versus the Dow, 2006-2009

a bad investment—but even if the options hadn't expired, I would have held on to them, leaving myself completely open to unsystematic as well as systematic risk.

It's hard to completely diversify away from market risk; when the overall market turns downward, certain parts of your portfolio are going to be hit. But the idea is that the other parts of your portfolio that are invested in different asset classes will augment the parts of your portfolio that took a dip.

And investing in several different asset classes and companies will allow you to diversify away from unsystematic risk like a company going bankrupt or being investigated for an accounting scandal.

As Figure 2.1 shows, if you had been invested in commodities—gold, in this example, during 2008, when the stock market crashed—you would have made a ton of money.

If you were properly diversified, you could have actually made money during the recent recession. Most "financial advisors" will try to tell you that being invested in a wide variety of equities (large cap, midcap, and small cap) and bonds is diversification enough.

Figure 2.1 shows that this simply is untrue. You need to be invested in stocks and bonds, as well as commodities (futures), currency (FOREX), cash, and volatility.

Volatility? As an asset class? Indeed. As the markets are flooded with small-time traders via online brokerage firms, large swings in prices are becoming more common.

A popular way to invest in volatility is through the simultaneous buying and selling of options on an asset—be it a stock, future, currency, or the volatility index (VIX). There are many different ways to do this, which I cover in detail throughout this book.

Another more complex way to invest in volatility is through variance swaps. This investment gives the trader a pure and perfect exposure to volatility of an asset. It's similar to a forward contract, yet it resembles a call option in many aspects.

Basically, the trader, or the holder of the swap, agrees to swap the realized volatility at the end of the tenure, with a strike level of volatility agreed at the initiation of the contract. It is a forward contract on future volatility entered today.

A defining feature of a volatility (variance) swap is that it is synthetically created, and it creates an exposure to a synthetic contract called the "log forward" or the "log contract" (natural logarithm of the forward or the spot price). A log contract, by its very construction, gives a 100 percent pure exposure to volatility of the underlying.

Even though a variance swap is priced as weighted portfolios of calls and puts, with weights being functions of strike levels, it gives a far greater—and purer—exposure to volatility of the underlying asset than options.

Types of Options and Pricing

If you are new to options investing, have no fear. In this section, I will go over all the basics of options. It's very important that you understand these basic concepts and terminology before we get into the more advanced strategies.

Call Options

When you purchase a call option, it gives you the right to buy a certain asset at a fixed price (the strike price) at any time before a specific expiration date. When you sell or write a call option, you assume the legal obligation to sell a certain asset at a specified strike price if the option is exercised before the expiration date.

By purchasing a call option, the investor is anticipating an appreciation of the underlying asset. By selling or writing a call option, the investor is anticipating a depreciation of the underlying asset.

Put Options

Put options are the exact opposite of call options. When you purchase a put, it gives you the right to sell a certain asset at the strike price anytime before the expiration date. When you sell or write a put option, you assume the legal obligation to purchase a certain asset at a specified strike price if the option is exercised before the expiration date.

By purchasing a put option, the investor is anticipating a depreciation of the underlying asset. By selling or writing a put option, the investor is anticipating an appreciation of the underlying asset.

The Underlying Asset

Stocks: There are around 2,000 stocks and indexes for which options are available in the United States.

Futures: This includes all the commodities, such as gold, silver, soy, wheat, oil, and many others.

Currency: Options are also available on most currencies traded on the FOREX market.

The VIX: This is the volatility index that tracks the implied volatility of the S&P 500.

Examples of Options

General Electric May 35 Call Option   The option buyer has the right to purchase 100 shares of General Electric at the strike price of $35 per share at any time before the option expires on the third Friday of May. If the buyer of the option decides to exercise the option, then the option writer (the seller) has the legal obligation to sell 100 shares of General Electric to the buyer at $35 per share.

Red Robin December 50 Put Option   The option buyer has the right to sell 100 shares of Red Robin at the strike price of $50 per share at any time before the option expires on the third Friday of December. If the buyer of the option decides to exercise the option, then the option writer (the seller) has the legal obligation to sell 100 shares of Red Robin to the buyer at $50 per share.

Why Purchase Options?

Investors purchase call and put options (often referred to as "going long") for two reasons—leverage and limited risk. When you buy an option, your risk is limited to the price you pay for the option. In terms of leverage, it allows the investor to control an expensive asset like gold for a fraction of what it would cost to purchase the asset outright.

Before you start investing in options, just beware that most people who trade options lose money. It is sad but true. And it is because they buy options, and that's all they do. They don't take advantage of other, more complex option strategies.

Almost 80 percent of all options expire worthless. The general investing public buys options without paying attention to the fair value of the option and the implied volatility. (I'll explain this later.) As a result, they purchase extremely overpriced options and often wind up losing money, even when they were correct about the price direction.

When you are finished reading this book, you will know how to take advantage of the factors that cause most people to lose money. You will learn how to put together safe yet powerful option strategies that make profits under all kinds of conditions.

In the Money

Call options that have a strike price below the current market price of the underlying asset are said to be in the money (ITM). Likewise, put options that have a strike price that is above the current market price of the underlying asset are in the money. For example, when Google is trading at $380, a Google November 370 call option (370 strike price) would be 10 points in the money, and a 390 put option would be 10 points in the money.

Out of the Money

This is the opposite of in the money. Call options that have a strike price that is above the current market price of the underlying asset are out of the money (OTM). Put options that have a strike price that is below the current market price of the underlying asset are out of the money. Continuing with the previous example, when Google is trading at $380, a Google November 370 call option would be 10 points out of the money, and a Google 390 put option would be 10 points out of the money.

At the Money

When an option's strike price is the same as the current market price, the option is at the money (ATM). Actually, whichever strike price is closest to the market price is considered to be at the money. Therefore, if General Electric's price is $13.50, the 14 call option and the 13 put option would both be considered at the money (even though the call option is technically half a point out of the money and the put option is half a point out of the money).

American Style versus European Style

American-style options can be exercised anytime before the expiration date. European-style options can only be exercised upon expiration (right before they expire). Most options that trade on exchanges in the United States are American style. However, many index options, like the SPX (S&P 500 index option), are European-style options.

Option Premium

This is simply the price of the option.

Each stock option covers 100 shares of stock. For example, when you see a stock option's price (premium) quoted at 2.50, it means that one option costs $2.50 per share times 100 shares, for a total cost of $250. So, for stock options, just multiply the quoted premium by 100 to get the total cost.

Options on futures contracts, index options, and so on each have their own specified quantities. For example, each soybean futures contract covers 5,000 bushels of soybeans, and the price is stated in cents per bushel. So, if an option on a soybean futures contract has a premium of 10, it means the cost of one option is 10 cents per bushel times 5,000 bushels, for a total cost of $500.

An option's premium consists of two components:

Intrinsic value: This is basically the amount that the option is in the money. For example, if Dell is trading at $40 and you hold a March 35 call, then the call has an intrinsic value of $5.

Time value: This is the additional amount that people are willing to pay over and above the intrinsic value. Time value equals the difference between the option's current price and the intrinsic value. So, if an option's premium is 4.25 and its intrinsic value is 3.50, the time value is 0.75.

Time Decay

The time value of an option's premium erodes as the option approaches the expiration date. Time decay accelerates and becomes most noticeable during the last month before expiration.

Exercising an Option

Call options: When you exercise a call option, you buy the underlying asset at the strike price, and you can then sell it at the current market price. For instance, suppose you own a McDonald's July 65 call option, and McDonald's stock is currently trading at $70. Exercising the call option, you would buy 100 shares of McDonald's at $65 and then sell the 100 shares at the current market price of $70. Your profit would be $5 per share, which was the intrinsic value of the option.

Put options: Now, this is a little different. First, you buy the underlying asset at the market price, and then you exercise the put option, selling the asset at the strike price. Let's say you own a McDonald's 75 put option, and you decide to exercise that option. First, you would need to buy 100 shares of McDonald's at the market price of $70. Next, you would exercise your put option, selling the 100 shares at the strike price of $75. Your profit would be $5 per share, which is the intrinsic value of the option.

Just remember that when you exercise an option, you only receive the intrinsic value. If the option still has time value, you would lose that profit. For this reason, investors normally don't exercise options that still have time value remaining.

In fact, only 2 percent of all options are ever exercised. Normally, when you buy an option, you will sell it before it expires (and take your profit or loss) or just let it expire worthless.

Understanding Options Greeks

Options Greeks symbols measure the options sensitivity to risk components inherent to the price of an option. They measure the speed of an underlying security's price movement, interest rate movement, time decay of an option, and volatility.

The Greeks are vital tools in risk management. Each Greek measures the sensitivity of the value of a portfolio to a small change in a given underlying parameter so that component risks may be treated in isolation, and the portfolio can be rebalanced accordingly to achieve a desired exposure.

Delta and gamma measure options sensitivity to the speed of price changes in the underlying security. Rho measures the options interest rate sensitivity. Theta measures the change in an options price due to change in the time left until expiration, and vega measures the change in an options price due to changes in the option's historical volatility.

The web site www.ivolatility.com provides an excellent free options pricing tool that will calculate all of the Greeks and volatility on any option you desire.

Delta

Delta measures the rate of change in the option price over the rate of change in the price of the underlying security. Therefore, we can say that delta measures the speed of the option price movement relative to a single-point move in the underlying security. Long calls and naked puts have positive delta, while short calls and long puts have negative delta.

$$\text{Delta} = (\text{rate of change in option price})/$$
$$(\text{rate of change in underlying security price})$$

If you owned a call option at \$2 when the stock was \$30 and the stock moved up to \$31, the option would move to \$2.50. In the preceding formula, the delta in this situation would be (\$2.50 − \$2)/(\$31 − \$30) = 0.5.

Conversely, let's say you owned a put at \$2 and the stock moved higher by 1 point, which resulted in the put option decreasing in value by \$0.50. The delta in this case would be (\$1.50 − \$2)/(\$31 − \$30) = −0.5.

The closer the delta is to 1 or −1, the greater the response is in the price of the option when the price of the underlying changes.

The preceding examples assumed that nothing else changed; however, in reality, changes in vega, theta, and rho can impact delta.

Delta Ranges for Calls and Puts   If an option is in the money, the delta for a call will approach 1, while the delta of a put will approach −1. At-the-money options will be near 0.5 and −0.5, while out-of-the-money options will have a delta value approaching zero as they move further out of the money. Also, remember that as the option comes closer to expiration, especially within 30 days, the delta curve becomes steeper; basically, the option becomes more sensitive to price movement in the underlying.

Delta Neutral Trading   Delta neutral trading, also known as "hedge" trading, is a method of trading where the total position delta is zero. The idea is to hedge your position by slowing your position speed down. Delta neutral trading is used by many traders to make profitable adjustments on their trade as the price of the security moves up and down. For example, a popular strategy is to make adjustments to your total position to bring it back to delta neutral after the underlying security has moved 20 percent in either direction. This can be done by making adjustments to the profitable side of your trade.

Let's create a simple example of a delta neutral trade. Assume we bought 100 shares of Microsoft, which would represent +100 deltas. We would need to either buy two at-the-money puts or sell two at-the-money calls *or* buy one at-the-money put and sell one at-the-money call. Either scenario would get you to delta neutral.

Remember, delta neutral does *not* mean that you have set up a risk-free position. It means that you have slowed down the speed of the percentage changes of your position.

Gamma

The delta of a stock relies on the price of the stock in relation to the strike price of the option. Therefore, when the stock price changes, so does the delta. This is where gamma becomes relevant. Gamma is an estimation of the change in delta for a 1 point move in a stock and can be thought of as the second derivative of delta.

A large gamma value indicates that delta will shift strongly as the underlying security moves up and down.

A long call and long put will have positive gamma, while the short counterparts will always be negative. A positive gamma refers to the idea that the delta of a long will become higher, or closer to 1, as the underlying security moves higher. The long put gamma will also move closer to −1 as the underlying security continues to move lower. The opposite can be said for short calls and short puts.

Gamma reaches its highest value when a stock is trading at the money or near the money. This value goes lower as the security moves further out of the money or further in the money. This makes logical sense, as the option price has the highest probability of moving from being OTM to ITM or ITM to OTM.

Theta

Theta represents the measure for time decay of an option. Remember, an option price consists of intrinsic value and time premium. Theta measures the decay in time premium as every day passes until expiration. Therefore, we can say that the theta for a long call or put will be negative, while the opposite can be said for the short call and put. This is true because when you are long an option, you will lose money in that option every day, all else being equal, due to the time premium decaying. However, the time decay in a short option will increase your profits.

Theta does not adjust evenly as time goes on. The closer and closer the option is to expiration, the greater the time decay will be. Theta will accelerate at a higher rate, especially when the option has less than 30 days to go. This also makes logical sense, because the option has less time to get or stay in a profitable situation. Additionally, an options theta will be highest when the stock is at the money. Since the stock has basically no intrinsic value, the time value component is the majority of the premium and will fluctuate strongly as expiration approaches.

Relationship between Theta and Gamma   There is a direct correlation between theta and gamma. When an options gamma is high, the theta moves higher as well. When I say higher, I mean theta becomes more negative, which negatively impacts the time premium for a long option holder. Some options traders will actually play the high theta by selling shorter-term options and buying that same strike option with a greater term to maturity at the same time. They are banking on the fact that the longer-dated option will have slower time decay than the shorter-dated option.

Rho

Rho measures theoretical option price changes due to interest rate shifts. While this measure of option price sensitivity is the least used, it has more relevant context when applied to higher-priced stocks. Why? Remember that a call option commands a large amount of stock with a relatively small amount of investment. Most times, the value of the underlying that the option commands is worth in excess of 10 times the value of the option itself. If you would have to buy the stock, you would need quite a bit more money, and the interest expense related to that amount is built into a call option premium. As you can see, as interest rates increase, a call option will increase in value, and a put option will decrease in value. It is for this reason that calls have a positive rho when interest rates rise. Conversely, if interest rates fall, put premiums will increase, while call premiums will decrease.

Vega

When an option position is established—either net buying or selling—the volatility dimension often gets overlooked by inexperienced traders, largely due to a lack of understanding. Like delta, which measures the sensitivity of an option to changes in the underlying price, vega is a risk measure of the sensitivity of an option price to changes in volatility.

The following table provides a summary of the vega sign (negative for short volatility and positive for long volatility) for all outright options positions and many complex strategies.

	Vega Sign	Increase in Implied Volatility	Decrease in Implied Volatility
Long Call	Positive	Gain	Loss
Short Call	Negative	Loss	Gain
Long Put	Positive	Gain	Loss
Short Put	Negative	Loss	Gain

When you own a call or a put (meaning you bought the option) and volatility declines, the price of the option will decline. This is obviously not beneficial and results in a loss for long calls and puts. On the other hand, short call and short put traders would experience a gain from the decline in volatility. Volatility will have an immediate impact, and the size of the price decline or gains will depend on the size of vega.

Simply put, a higher vega results in higher option prices. This is because higher volatility gives the option a better chance to expire in the money. Most novice options traders understand that the price of the underlying asset and the time until expiration affect the price of options, but many overlook or just don't realize that volatility plays a very crucial role as well.

Valuing Volatility

As an essential element in determining the level of option prices, volatility is a measure of the rate and magnitude of the change of prices (up or down) of the underlying asset. If volatility is high, the premium on the option will be relatively high, and vice versa. Once you have a measure of historical volatility (HV) for any underlying, you can plug the value into a standard options pricing model and calculate the fair market value of an option.

A model's fair market value, however, is often out of line with the actual market value for that same option. This is known as option mispricing and is caused by an option's implied volatility (IV).

Option pricing models calculate implied volatility using historical volatility and current market prices. For instance, if the price of an option should be 3 points in premium price and the option price today is at 4, the additional premium is attributed to implied volatility.

When volatility is high, meaning implied volatility is higher than historical volatility (IV > HV), the options are overvalued compared to fair market value. You want to sell options that are overvalued in anticipation of volatility dropping and returning to its normal, historical volatility.

On the other hand, when volatility is low, meaning implied volatility is lower than historical volatility (IV < HV), the options are undervalued, and this is when you want to buy or go long an option.

Keep in mind that both IV and HV tend to revert to their normally lower levels and can do so quite quickly. You can, therefore, have a sudden collapse of IV (and HV) and a quick fall in premiums, even without a move in the underlying asset price. This is where most novice options traders get cleaned out.

It is a good idea to get in the habit of checking the levels of volatility (both HV and IV) before establishing any option position. It is worth investing in some good software to make the job easy and accurate.

To summarize, volatility is a measure of how rapid price changes have been (HV) and what the market expects the price to do (IV). When implied volatility is high, buyers of options should be wary of straight options buying, and they should be looking instead to sell options. Low implied volatility, on the other hand, which generally occurs in quiet markets, will offer better prices for buyers; however, there's no guarantee the market will make a violent move anytime soon. By incorporating an awareness of IV and HV, which are important dimensions of pricing, you can gain a serious edge as an options trader.

Determining What Options Strategy to Use and When

Now that you have a good understanding of options volatility and how it affects price, we can get into the meat of the book: advanced options strategies aimed at making you money in any market environment.

Before you start trading, you will need to acquire some sort of options pricing program so that you can calculate Greeks and volatility. I use OptionsVue, which I highly recommend because of all of its additional analytical and charting features, but you can also find free programs on the Internet that do the basics, such as at www.ivolatility.com.

Remember that no matter which way the stock market is going—up, down, or sideways—it never travels in a straight line. The market is constantly oscillating. So, having a wide variety of trading techniques that augment gains and take advantage of volatility will always be of use.

It's up to you to determine what underlying asset you want to invest in. I like to screen for high beta stocks with average six-month price fluctuations exceeding 20 percent and then go through the options and calculate volatility. I sell options that have a higher implied volatility than historical volatility, and I buy options that have a lower implied volatility than historical volatility.

Conclusion

In this chapter, we covered all the options basics, from what an option is to the importance of volatility in derivatives trading.

In the next three chapters, I will outline advanced option strategies that you can use to exploit volatility in bull markets, bear markets, and pig (or sideways) markets. You can apply these strategies to index exchange-traded funds (ETFs) and play the direction of the overall market, or you can use them with equities and commodities options.

When we're done with the advanced options strategies, I will go into detail about the commodities, FOREX, single stock futures, and international investing markets. These are all markets that provide a great outlet for options trading, and some of these markets provide margin accounts of up to 100:1—much higher than the 2:1 margin that you get with equities.

CHAPTER 3

Beating the Bulls

How can you augment and hedge yourself when you are antici-pating a bull run in an underlying asset, be it the overall market, an individual stock, commodity, or currency? In this chapter, I will go over several options techniques, all of which you can use to take advantage of bullish market situations.

Keep in mind that it is beneficial to try to assess the possible price increase and the time frame in which the rally will occur in order to select the most appropriate trading strategy. I will also use the following abbreviations when describing price: ATM (at the money), ITM (in the money), and OTM (out of the money).

The most bullish of the options trading strategies is the simple call buying strategy used by most novice options traders.

In most cases, stocks seldom go up by leaps and bounds. Moderately bullish options traders usually set a target price for the bull run and utilize bull spreads to reduce risk. While maximum profit is capped for these strategies, they usually cost less to employ.

Mildly bullish trading strategies are options strategies that make money as long as the underlying stock price does not go down on the options expiration date. These strategies usually provide a small downside protection as well. Writing out-of-the-money covered calls is one example of such a strategy.

Speculation Techniques in Bull Markets

Long Call

Long Call Composition

Buy 1 ATM Call

When to use: When you are bullish on market direction and also bullish on market volatility.

A long call option is the simplest way to benefit if you believe that the market will make an upward move and is the most common choice among first-time investors.

A long call option means that you will benefit if the stock/future rallies, and your risk is limited on the downside if the market makes a correction.

From the graph shown in Figure 3.1, you can see that if the stock/future is below the stock price at expiration, your only loss will be the premium paid for the option. Even if the stock goes into liquidation, you will never lose more than the option premium that you paid initially at the trade date.

Not only will your losses be limited on the downside, but you will also still benefit infinitely if the market stages a strong rally. A long call has unlimited profit potential on the upside. (See Figure 3.1.)

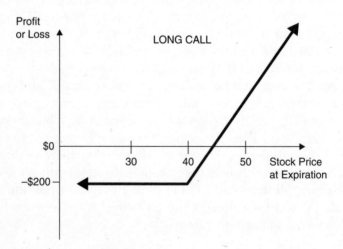

Figure 3.1   Long Call Strategy

Example   Suppose the stock of XYZ Company is trading at $40. A call option contract with a strike price of $40 expiring in a month's time is being priced at $2. You believe that XYZ stock will rise sharply in the coming weeks, and so you paid $200 to purchase a single $40 XYZ call option covering 100 shares.

Say you were proven right and the price of XYZ stock rallies to $50 on option expiration date. With the underlying stock price at $50, if you were to exercise your call option, you invoke your right to buy 100 shares of XYZ stock at $40 each and can sell them immediately in the open market for $50 a share. This gives you a profit of $10 per share. As each call option contract covers 100 shares, the total amount you will receive from the exercise is $1,000. Since you had paid $200 to purchase the call option, your net profit for the entire trade is therefore $800.

However, if you were wrong in your assessment and the stock price had instead dived to $30, your call option will expire worthless, and your total loss will be the $200 that you paid to purchase the option.

Unlimited Profit Potential   Since there is no limit as to how high the stock price can be at expiration date, there is no limit to the maximum profit possible when implementing the long call option strategy.

The formula for calculating profit is given next:

$$\text{Maximum profit} = \text{unlimited}$$

Profit achieved when price of underlying
$\geq$ strike price of long call + premium paid

$$\text{Profit} = \text{price of underlying} - \text{strike price of long call} - \text{premium paid}$$

Limited Risk   Risk for the long call options strategy is limited to the price paid for the call option, no matter how low the stock price is trading on the expiration date.

The formula for calculating maximum loss is given next:

$$\text{Max loss} = \text{premium paid} + \text{commissions paid}$$

Max loss occurs when price of underlying $\leq$ strike price of long call

Breakeven Point(s)   The underlier price at which breakeven is achieved for the long call position can be calculated using the following formula:

$$\text{Breakeven point} = \text{strike price of long call} + \text{premium paid}$$

Summary   Compared to buying the underlying shares outright, the call option buyer is able to gain leverage, since the lower-priced calls appreciate in value faster percentagewise for every point rise in the price of the underlying stock.

However, call options have a limited lifespan. If the underlying stock price does not move above the strike price before the option expiration date, the call option will expire worthless.

Naked Put

Naked Put Composition

Sell 1 ATM Put

When to use: When you are bullish on market direction and bearish on market volatility.

Selling naked puts can be a very risky strategy, as your losses are unlimited in a falling market.

Although selling puts carries the potential for unlimited losses on the downside, they are a great way to position yourself to buy stock when it becomes cheap. Selling a put option is another way of saying, "I would buy this stock for [strike] price if it were to trade there by [expiration] date."

A short put locks in the purchase price of a stock at the strike price. Plus, you will keep any premium received as a result of the trade. (See Figure 3.2.)

Example   Suppose XYZ stock is trading at $45 in June. An options trader writes an uncovered JUL 45 put for $200.

If XYZ stock rallies to $50 on expiration, the JUL 45 put expires worthless, and the trader gets to keep the $200 in premium as profit. This is also his or her maximum profit and is achieved as long as XYZ stock trades above $45 on options expiration date.

If instead, XYZ stock drops to $40 on expiration, then the JUL 45 put expires in the money, with $500 in intrinsic value. The JUL

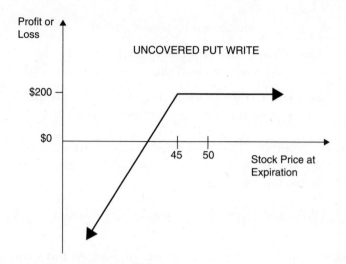

Figure 3.2   Uncovered Put Write

45 put needs to be bought back for $500, and subtracting the initial credit of $200 taken, the resulting net loss is $300.

Limited Profits with No Upside Risk   Profit for the uncovered put write is limited to the premiums received for the options sold, and unlike the covered put write, since the uncovered put writer is not short on the underlying stock, he or she does not have to bear any loss should the price of the security go up at expiration. The naked put writer sells slightly out-of-the-money puts month after month, collecting premiums as long as the stock price of the underlying remains above the put strike price at expiration.

The formula for calculating maximum profit is given next:

$$\text{Max profit} = \text{premium received} - \text{commissions paid}$$

Max profit achieved when price of underlying
$\geq$ strike price of short put

Unlimited Downside Risk with Little Downside Protection   While the premium collected can cushion a slight drop in stock price, loss resulting from a catastrophic drop in stock price of the underlying can be huge when implementing the uncovered put write strategy.

The formula for calculating loss is given next:

$$\text{Maximum loss} = \text{unlimited}$$

Loss occurs when price of underlying
$< \text{strike price of short put} - \text{premium received}$

$\text{Loss} = \text{strike price of short put} - \text{price of underlying}$
$- \text{premium received} + \text{commissions paid}$

Breakeven Point(s)   The underlier price at which breakeven is achieved for the uncovered put write position can be calculated using the following formula:

$$\text{Breakeven point} = \text{strike price of short put} - \text{premium received}$$

Summary   The biggest risk facing the uncovered put writer is that should the price of the underlying drop below the put strike price, he or she is forced to buy the shares at the put strike price. However, for a long-term investor looking to go long on the stock at a discount, writing naked puts can be a great way to buy stock. He or she can do that by writing uncovered puts with a strike price at or near his or her target entry price. If the stock price drops below the put strike and the puts get assigned, he or she gets to make the stock purchase at the desired price.

Additionally, he or she gets a further discount in the form of the premium earned from selling the puts. Even if the put strike price was not reached and the stock not acquired, he or she still gets to keep the premiums!

Bull Call Spread

Bull Call Spread Composition

Buy 1 ITM Call
Sell 1 OTM Call

When to use: When you are mildly bullish on market price and/or volatility.

You can see from the graph in Figure 3.3 that a call bull spread can only be worth as much as the difference between the two strike prices. So, when putting on a bull spread, remember that the wider the strikes are, the more you can make. The downside to this is that you will end up paying more for the spread. Therefore, the deeper in-the-money calls you buy relative to the call options that you sell means a greater maximum loss if the market sells off.

Like I mentioned, a call bull spread is a very cost-effective way to take a position when you are bullish on market direction. The cost of the bought call option will be partially offset by the premium received by the sold call option. This does, however, limit your potential gain if the market does rally but also reduces the cost of entering into this position.

This type of strategy is suited to investors who want to go long on market direction and also have an upside target in mind. The sold call acts as a profit target for the position. So, if the trader sees a short-term move in an underlying but doesn't see the market going past X dollars, then a bull spread is ideal. With a bull spread, he or she can easily go long without the added expenditure of an outright long stock and can even reduce the cost by selling the additional call option. (See Figure 3.3.)

Example   An options trader believes that XYZ stock trading at $42 is going to rally soon and enters a bull call spread by buying a JUL 40 call for $300 and writing a JUL 45 call for $100. The net investment required to put on the spread is a debit of $200.

The stock price of XYZ begins to rise and closes at $46 on expiration date. Both options expire in the money, with the JUL 40 call having an intrinsic value of $600 and the JUL 45 call having an

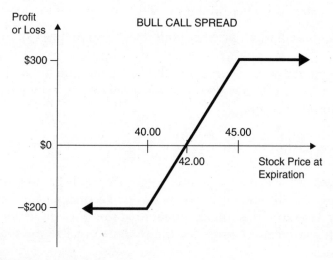

Figure 3.3 Bull Call Spread

intrinsic value of $100. This means that the spread is now worth $500 at expiration. Since the trader had a debit of $200 when he or she bought the spread, his or her net profit is $300.

If the price of XYZ had declined to $38 instead, both options expire worthless. The trader will lose his or her entire investment of $200, which is also his or her maximum possible loss.

Limited Upside Profits   Maximum gain is reached for the bull call spread options strategy when the stock price moves above the higher-strike price of the two calls, and it is equal to the difference between the strike prices of the two call options minus the initial debit taken to enter the position.

The formula for calculating maximum profit is given next:

$$\text{Max profit} = \text{strike price of short call} - \text{strike price of long call} \\ - \text{net premium paid} - \text{commissions paid}$$

$$\text{Max profit achieved when price of underlying} \\ \geq \text{strike price of short call}$$

Limited Downside Risk   The bull call spread strategy will result in a loss if the stock price declines at expiration. Maximum loss cannot be more than the initial debit taken to enter the spread position.

The formula for calculating maximum loss is given next:

$$\text{Max loss} = \text{net premium paid} + \text{commissions paid}$$

$$\text{Max loss occurs when price of underlying} \leq \text{strike price of long call}$$

Breakeven Point(s)   The underlier price at which breakeven is achieved for the bull call spread position can be calculated using the following formula:

$$\text{Breakeven point} = \text{strike price of long call} + \text{net premium paid}$$

Summary   One can enter a more aggressive bull spread position by widening the difference between the strike prices of the two call options. However, this will also mean that the stock price must move upward by a greater degree for the trader to realize the maximum profit.

Bull Put Spread

Bull Put Spread Composition
Buy 1 OTM Put
Sell 1 ITM Put

When to use: When you are bullish on market and/or volatility.

A put bull spread has the same payoff as the call bull spread, except the contracts used are put options instead of call options. Even though bullish, a trader may decide to place a put spread instead of a call spread, because the risk/reward profile may be more favorable. This may be the case if the ITM call options have a higher implied volatility than the OTM put options. In this case, a call spread would be more expensive to initiate, and hence the trader might prefer the lower-cost option of a put spread. (See Figure 3.4.)

Example An options trader believes that XYZ stock trading at $43 is going to rally soon and enters a bull put spread by buying a JUL 40 put for $100 and writing a JUL 45 put for $300. Thus, the trader receives a net credit of $200 when entering the spread position.

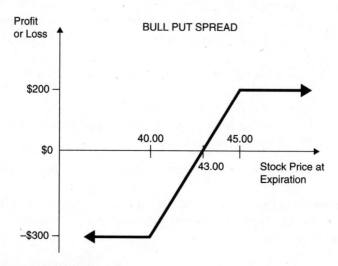

Figure 3.4 Bull Put Spread

The stock price of XYZ begins to rise and closes at $46 on expiration date. Both options expire worthless, and the options trader keeps the entire credit of $200 as profit, which is also the maximum profit possible.

If the price of XYZ had instead declined to $38, both options expire in the money, with the JUL 40 call having an intrinsic value of $200 and the JUL 45 call having an intrinsic value of $700.

This means that the spread is now worth $500 at expiration. Since the trader had received a credit of $200 when he or she entered the spread, his or her net loss comes to $300. This is also his or her maximum possible loss.

Limited Upside Profit   If the stock price closes above the higher-strike price on expiration date, both options expire worthless, and the bull put spread option strategy earns the maximum profit, which is equal to the credit taken in when entering the position.

The formula for calculating maximum profit is given next:

$$\text{Max profit} = \text{net premium received} - \text{commissions paid}$$

$$\text{Max profit achieved when price of underlying} \geq \text{strike price of short put}$$

Limited Downside Risk   If the stock price drops below the lower-strike price on expiration date, then the bull put spread strategy incurs a maximum loss equal to the difference between the strike prices of the two puts minus the net credit received when putting on the trade.

The formula for calculating maximum loss is given next:

$$\text{Max loss} = \text{strike price of short put}$$
$$- \text{strike price of long put net premium received}$$
$$+ \text{commissions paid}$$

Max loss occurs when price of underlying ≤ strike price of long put

Breakeven Point(s)   The underlier price at which breakeven is achieved for the bull put spread position can be calculated using the following formula:

Breakeven point = strike price of short put − net premium received

Summary When your feeling on a stock is generally positive, bull spreads are nice, low-risk, low-reward strategies. One way to create a bull spread that you might not immediately consider is by using put options at or near the current market price of the stock.

Call Backspread

Call Backspread Composition

Sell 1 ITM Call
Buy 2 OTM Calls

When to use: When you are bullish on volatility and bullish on market price. Note, though, that you profit when prices fall, although the gains are greater if the market rallies.

A backspread looks a lot like a long straddle, except the payoff flattens out on the downside. The other key difference is that backspreads are usually done at a credit. That is, the net difference for both legs means that you receive money into your account up front instead of paying (debit) for the spread.

Even though the payoff looks like a long-type position, it is often referred to as a short strategy. Generally, it is like this: If you receive money for the position up front, it is called a short position; when you pay for a position, it is called long. (See Figure 3.5.)

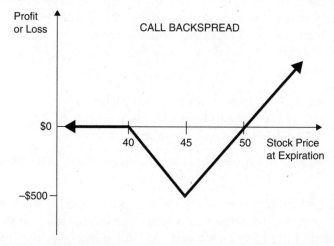

Figure 3.5   Call Backspread

Example   Suppose XYZ stock is trading at $43 in June. An options trader executes a 2:1 call backspread by selling a JUL 40 call for $400 and buying two JUL 45 calls for $200 each. The net debit/credit taken to enter the trade is zero.

On expiration in July, if XYZ stock is trading at $45, both the JUL 45 calls expire worthless, while the short JUL 40 call expires in the money, with $500 in intrinsic value. Buying back this call to close the position will result in the maximum loss of $500 for the options trader.

If XYZ stock rallies and is trading at $50 on expiration in July, all the options will expire in the money. The short JUL 40 call is worth $1,000 and needs to be bought back to close the position. Since the two JUL 45 calls bought are now worth $500 each, their combined value of $1,000 is just enough to offset the losses from the written call. Therefore, he or she achieves breakeven at $50.

Beyond $50, though, there will be no limit to the gains possible. For example, at $60, each long JUL 45 call will be worth $1,500, while his or her single short JUL 40 call is only worth $2,000, resulting in a profit of $1,000.

If the stock price had dropped to $40 or below at expiration, all the options involved would expire worthless. Since the net debit to put on this trade is zero, there is no resulting loss.

Unlimited Profit Potential   The call backspread profits when the stock price makes a strong move to the upside beyond the upper breakeven point. There is no limit to the maximum possible profit.

The formula for calculating profit is given next:

$$\text{Maximum profit} = \text{unlimited}$$

Profit achieved when price of underlying
$\geq 2 \times$ strike price of long call − strike price of short call
$\pm$ net premium paid/received

Profit = price of underlying − strike price of long call − max loss

Limited Risk   Maximum loss for the call backspread is limited and is taken when the underlying stock price at expiration is at the strike price of the long calls purchased. At this price, both the long calls expire worthless, while the short call expires in the money. Maximum loss is equal to the intrinsic value of the short call plus or minus any debit or credit taken when putting on the spread.

The formula for calculating maximum loss is given next:

$$\text{Max loss} = \text{strike price of long call} - \text{strike price of short call} \\ \pm \text{net premium paid/received} + \text{commissions paid}$$

Breakeven Point(s)   There are two break even points for the call backspread position. The breakeven points can be calculated using the following formulae:

$$\text{Upper breakeven point} = \text{strike price of long call} \\ + \text{points of maximum loss}$$

$$\text{Lower breakeven point} = \text{strike price of short call}$$

Summary   Call backspreads are great strategies when you are expecting big moves in already-volatile stocks. To maximize the potential for this position, many traders use in-the-money options, because they have a higher likelihood of finishing in the money.

Hedging Techniques in Bull Markets

The techniques just outlined are mainly used for pure speculation, as a separate investment to play volatility and augment profits in bull markets. However, when you actually own the underlying asset, you can use the following hedging strategies to magnify profits and reduce risk in a bullish environment.

The Collar

Collar Composition
Long 100 Shares
Sell 1 OTM Call
Buy 1 OTM Put

When to use: If you own the underlying asset and are very bullish on volatility.

As you can see from Figure 3.6, a collar behaves just like a long call spread.

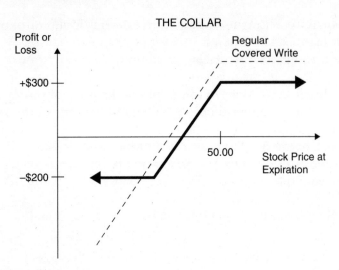

Figure 3.6   The Collar

It is suited to investors who already own the stock and are looking to (1) increase their return by writing call options and (2) minimize their downside risk by buying put options.

Covered calls are becoming a very popular strategy for investors who already own stock. They sell out-of-the-money call options at a price that they are happy to sell the stock for in return for receiving some premium up front. If the stock doesn't trade above this level, the investor keeps the premium.

If the net premium is a credit—that is, you received money for the option legs—then your maximum gain is the difference between the strikes plus this amount (and then plus the profit from the stock leg). If the net premium was a payment, then it is subtracted from the strike differential. (See Figure 3.6.)

Example   Suppose an options trader is holding 100 shares of the stock XYZ that is currently trading at $48 in June. He or she decides to establish a collar by writing a JUL 50 covered call for $2 while simultaneously purchasing a JUL 45 put for $1.

Since he or she pays $4,800 for the 100 shares of XYZ and another $100 for the put but receives $200 for selling the call option, his or her total investment is $4,700.

On expiration date, the stock had rallied by 5 points to $53. Since the striking price of $50 for the call option is lower than the trading price of the stock, the call is assigned, and the trader sells the shares for $5,000, resulting in a $300 profit ($5,000 minus $4,700 original investment).

However, what happens should the stock price go down 5 points to $43 instead? Let's take a look.

At $43, the call writer would have had incurred a paper loss of $500 for holding the 100 shares of XYZ, but because of the JUL 45 protective put, he or she is able to sell his or her shares for $4,500 instead of $4,300. Thus, his or her net loss is limited to only $200 ($4,500 minus $4,700 original investment).

Had the stock price remain stable at $48 at expiration, he or she will still net a paper gain of $100 since he or she only paid a total of $4,700 to acquire $4,800 worth of stock.

Limited Profit Potential   The formula for calculating maximum profit is given next:

$$\text{Max profit} = \text{strike price of short call} - \text{purchase price of underlying} \\ + \text{net premium received} - \text{commissions paid}$$

$$\text{Max profit achieved when price of underlying} \\ \geq \text{strike price of short call}$$

Limited Risk   The formula for calculating maximum loss is given next:

$$\text{Max loss} = \text{purchase price of underlying} - \text{strike price of long put} \\ - \text{net premium received} + \text{commissions paid}$$

$$\text{Max loss occurs when price of underlying} \leq \text{strike price of long put}$$

Breakeven Point(s)   The underlier price at which breakeven is achieved for the collar strategy position can be calculated using the following formula:

$$\text{Breakeven point} = \text{purchase price of underlying} \\ + \text{net premium paid}$$

Summary   The beauty of using a collar strategy is that you know, right from the start, the potential losses and gains on a trade. While your returns are likely to be somewhat muted in an explosive bull market due to selling the call, on the flip side, should the stock head south, you'll have the comfort of knowing you're protected.

If capital protection rather than premium collection is the main focus, a bullish investor can establish an alternative collar strategy known as the costless collar.

The Costless Collar

Costless Collar Composition
Long 100 Shares
Sell 1 OTM LEAPS Call
Buy 1 ATM LEAPS Put

When to use: When you own the underlying asset and you are very bullish on volatility.

Costless collars can be established to fully protect existing long stock positions with little or no cost, since the premium paid for the protective puts is offset by the premiums received for writing the covered calls.

Depending on the volatility of the underlying, the call strike can range from 30 percent to 70 percent out of the money, enabling the writer of the call to still enjoy a limited profit should the stock price head north. This strategy is typically executed using LEAPS (a fancy name for options with expiration dates of a couple of years instead of a few months), as the striking price of the call sold can be rather high in relation to the price of the underlying stock. (See Figure 3.7.)

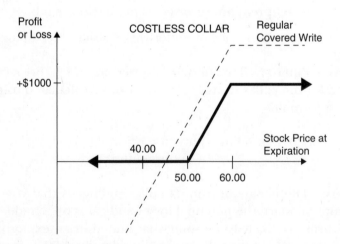

Figure 3.7   Costless Collar

Example Suppose the stock XYZ is currently trading at $50 in June 2006. An options trader holding on to 100 shares of XYZ wishes to protect his or her shares should the stock price take a dive. At the same time, he or she wants to hang on to the shares, as he or she feels that they will appreciate in the next 6 to 12 months. He or she sets up a costless collar by writing a one-year JUL 2007 60 LEAPS call for $5 while simultaneously using the proceeds from the call sale to buy a one-year JUL 2007 50 LEAPS put for $5.

If the stock price rallies to $70 at expiration date, his or her maximum profit is capped, as he or she is obliged to sell his or her shares at the strike price of $60. At 100 shares, his or her profit is $1,000.

On the other hand, should the stock price plunge to $40 instead, his or her loss is zero, since the protective put allows him or her to still sell his or her shares at $50.

However, should the stock price remain unchanged at $50, while his or her net loss is still zero, he or she would have "lost" one year's worth of premiums of $500 that would have been collected if not for the protective put purchase.

Summary By setting up the costless collar, a long-term stockholder forgoes any profit should the stock price appreciate beyond the striking price of the call written. In return, however, maximum downside protection is assured. As such, it is a good options strategy to use, especially for retirement accounts, where capital preservation is paramount.

Many senior executives at publicly traded companies who have large positions in their company's stock utilize costless collars as a way to protect their personal wealth. By using the zero-cost collar strategy, an executive can insure the value of his or her stock for years without having to pay high premiums for the insurance of the put.

Covered Call

Covered Call Composition
Long 100 Shares
Sell 1 OTM Call

When to use: When you own the underlying stock (or futures contract) and wish to lock in profits.

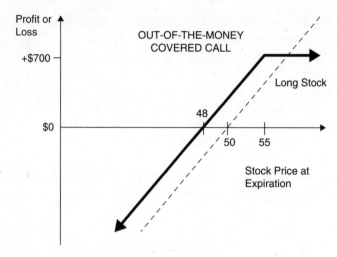

Figure 3.8   Out-of-the-Money Covered Call

This strategy is used by many investors who hold stock. It is also used by many large funds as a method of generating consistent income from the sold options.

The idea behind a covered call (also called a covered write) is to hold stock over a long period of time and every month or more sell out-of-the-money call options to collect income. This strategy is often used by advisory services that promote option strategies for generating monthly income while protecting capital. (See Figure 3.8.)

Example   An options trader purchases 100 shares of XYZ stock trading at $50 in June and writes a JUL 55 out-of-the-money call for $2. So, he or she pays $5,000 for the 100 shares of XYZ and receives $200 for writing the call option, giving a total investment of $4,800.

On expiration date, the stock had rallied to $57. Since the striking price of $55 for the call option is lower than the current trading price, the call is assigned, and the writer sells the shares for a $500 profit. This brings his or her total profit to $700 after factoring in the $200 in premiums received for writing the call.

It is interesting to note that the buyer of the call option in this case has a net profit of zero, even though the stock had gone up by 7 points.

However, what would have happened if the stock price had gone down 7 points to $43 instead? Let's take a look.

At \$43, the call writer will incur a paper loss of \$700 for holding the 100 shares of XYZ. However, his or her loss is offset by the \$200 in premiums received, so his or her total loss is \$500. In comparison, the call buyer's loss is limited to the premiums paid, which is \$200.

Limited Profit Potential   In addition to the premium received for writing the call, the OTM covered call strategy's profit also includes a paper gain if the underlying stock price rises, up to the strike price of the call option sold.

The formula for calculating maximum profit is given next:

$$\text{Max profit} = \text{premium received} - \text{purchase price of underlying} + \text{strike price of short call} - \text{commissions paid}$$

$$\text{Max profit achieved when price of underlying} \geq \text{strike price of short call}$$

Unlimited Loss Potential   Potential losses for this strategy can be very large and occur when the price of the underlying security falls. However, this risk is no different from that which the typical stock-owner is exposed to. In fact, the covered call writer's loss is cushioned slightly by the premiums received for writing the calls.

The formula for calculating loss is given next:

$$\text{Maximum loss} = \text{unlimited}$$

$$\text{Loss occurs when price of underlying} < \text{purchase price of underlying} - \text{premium received}$$

$$\text{Loss} = \text{purchase price of underlying} - \text{price of underlying} - \text{max profit} + \text{commissions paid}$$

Breakeven Point(s)   The underlier price at which breakeven is achieved for the covered call position can be calculated using the following formula:

$$\text{Breakeven point} = \text{purchase price of underlying} - \text{premium received}$$

Summary   Overall, writing out-of-the-money covered calls is an excellent strategy to use if you are mildly bullish toward the underlying stock, as they allow you to earn a premium, which also acts as a cushion should the stock price go down. So, if you are planning to hold on to the shares, anyway, and have a target selling price in mind that is not too far off, you should write a covered call.

Protective Put

Protective Put Composition

Long 100 Shares
Buy 1 ATM Put

When to use: When you own long stock and want to protect yourself against a market correction.

A protective put strategy has a very similar payoff profile to the long call. Your maximum loss is limited to the premium paid for the option, and you have an unlimited profit potential.

Protective puts are ideal for investors who are very risk averse; that is, they hold stock and are concerned about a stock market correction. If the market does sell off rapidly, the value of the put options that the trader holds will increase, while the value of the stock will decrease. If the combined position is hedged, then the profits of the put options will offset the losses of the stock, and all the investor will lose will be the premium paid.

However, if the market rises substantially past the exercise price of the put options, then the puts will expire worthless, while the stock position increases. But the loss of the put position is limited, while the profits gained from the increase in the stock position are unlimited. In this case, the losses of the put option and the gains from the stock do not offset each other: The profits gained from the increase in the underlying outweigh the loss sustained from the put option premium. (See Figure 3.9.)

Example An options trader owns 100 shares of XYZ stock trading at $50 in June. He or she implements a protective put strategy by purchasing a SEP 50 put option priced at $200 to insure his or her long stock position against a possible crash.

Maximum loss occurs when the stock price is $50 or lower at expiration. Even if the stock price nosedived to $30 on expiration, his or her max loss is capped at $200. Let's see how this works out.

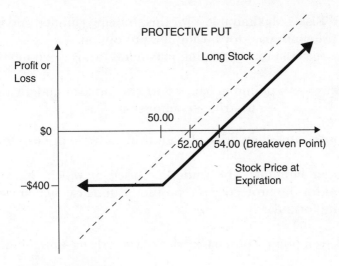

Figure 3.9 Protective Put

At $30, his or her long stock position will suffer a loss of $2,000. However, his or her SEP 50 put will have an intrinsic value of $2,000 and can be sold for that amount. Including the initial $200 paid to buy the put option, his or her net loss will be $2,000 − $2,000 + $200 = $200.

There is no limit to the profits attainable should the stock price go up. Suppose the stock price rallies to $70; his or her long stock position will gain $2,000. Excluding the $200 paid for the protective put, his or her net profit is $1,800.

Unlimited Profit Potential   There is no limit to the maximum profit attainable using this strategy. The protective put is also known as a synthetic long call, because its risk/reward profile is the same as that of a long call's profile.

The formula for calculating profit is given next:

$$\text{Maximum profit} = \text{unlimited}$$

Profit achieved when price of underlying
> purchase price of underlying + premium paid

Profit = price of underlying − purchase price of underlying
− premium paid

Limited Risk   Maximum loss for this strategy is limited and is equal to the premium paid for buying the put option.

The formula for calculating maximum loss is given next:

$$\text{Max loss} = \text{premium paid} + \text{purchase price of underlying} \\ - \text{put strike} + \text{commissions paid}$$

Max loss occurs when price of underlying $\leq$ strike price of long put

Breakeven Point(s)   The underlier price at which breakeven is achieved for the protective put position can be calculated using the following formula:

$$\text{Breakeven point} = \text{purchase price of underlying} + \text{premium paid}$$

Summary   With the market volatility we've seen over the past few years, more investors are recognizing the value of using puts as part of their everyday trading strategy.

For investors who put money in the volatile Internet or biotech sectors, the rewards can be enormous. But so can the risks; if the stock price rises instead of falls, this strategy may limit the upside potential by the cost of the put. By adding put options to their overall investment strategy, investors can better position themselves for any direction the market may head.

Stock Repair Spread

Stock Repair Spread Composition
Buy 1 ATM Call
Sell 2 OTM Calls

When to use: As an alternative strategy to recover from a loss after a long stock position has suffered from a drop in the stock price.

The stock repair strategy involves the implementation of a call ratio spread to reduce the breakeven price of a losing long stock position, thereby increasing the chance of fully recovering from the loss.

The most straightforward way to try to rescue a losing long stock position is to hold on to the shares and hope that the stock price

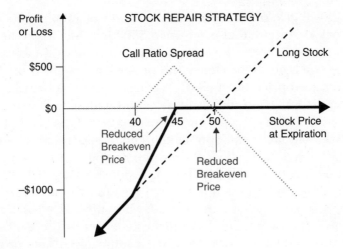

Figure 3.10 Stock Repair Strategy

returns to the original purchase price. However, this approach may take a long time (if ever).

To increase the likelihood of achieving breakeven, another common strategy is to double down and reduce the average purchase price. This method reduces the breakeven price, but there is a need to pump in additional funds, hence increasing downside risk.

The stock repair strategy, on the other hand, is able to reduce the breakeven at virtually no cost and with no additional downside risk. The only downside to this strategy is that the best it can do is to breakeven. This means that in the event that the stock rebounds sharply, the trader does not stand to make any additional profit. (See Figure 3.10.)

Example Suppose a trader had bought 100 shares of XYZ stock at $50 a share in May, but the price of the stock had since declined to $40 a month later, leaving him or her with a paper loss of $1,000. The trader decides to employ a stock repair strategy by implementing a 2:1 ratio call spread, buying a JUL 40 call for $200 and selling two JUL 45 calls for $100 each. The net debit/credit taken to enter the spread is zero.

On expiration in July, if XYZ stock is trading at $45, both the JUL 45 calls expire worthless, while the long JUL 40 call expires in the money, with $500 in intrinsic value. Selling or exercising this long call will give the options trader a profit of $500. As his or her long stock position has also regained $500 in value, his or her total gain comes to $1,000, which is equal to his or her initial loss from the long stock position. Hence, he or she has achieved breakeven at the reduced price of $45 and "repaired" his or her stock.

If XYZ stock rebounded strongly and is trading at $60 on expiration in July, all the call options will expire in the money, but as the trader has sold more call options than he or she has purchased, he or she will need to buy back the written calls at a loss. Each JUL 45 call written is now worth $1,500, but his or her long JUL 40 call is only worth $2,000 and is not enough to offset the losses from the written calls. This means that the trader has suffered a loss of $1,000 from the call ratio spread, but this loss is offset by the $2,000 gain from his or her long stock position, resulting in a net "profit" of $1,000—the amount of his or her initial loss before the stock repair move. Hence, with the stock price at $60, the trader still only achieved breakeven.

However, there is no additional downside risk to this repair strategy, and losses from a further drop in stock price will be no different from the losses suffered if the trader had simply held on to the shares. If the stock price had dropped to $30 or below at expiration, then all the options involved will expire worthless, so there will be no additional loss from the call ratio spread. However, the long stock position will still take on a further loss of $1,000.

Conclusion

In this chapter, we covered a wide variety of ways for an investor to compound gains in bull markets while also minding volatility. We covered techniques that you can use if you own the underlying stock (hedging), and we covered techniques that you can use when you don't own the underlying asset (speculation).

Keep in mind that just because you are making a lot of money in bull markets doesn't mean that the market isn't going to turn on you. If we learned anything from the tech bubble and credit crisis, it is that it's important to hedge your bets.

4

Taming the Bears

Market turndowns are inevitable. With every bull comes a bear. When the stock market is going up, it never follows a straight line—it zig zags; it just so happens that the ups are wider than the downs.

This chapter will cover a number of strategies that will give you the potential to make tons of money in these downturns.

The most bearish of options trading strategies is the simple put buying strategy utilized by most novice options traders.

In most cases, stock prices seldom make steep downward moves. Moderately bearish options traders usually set a target price for the expected decline and utilize bear spreads to reduce risk. While maximum profit is capped for these strategies, they usually cost less to employ.

Speculation Techniques in Bear Markets

Long Put

Long Put Composition
Buy 1 ATM Put

When to use: When you are bearish on market direction and bullish on market volatility.

Like the long call, a long put is a nice, simple way to take a position on market direction without risking everything. Except with a put option, you want the market to decrease in value.

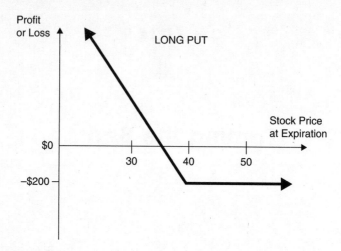

Figure 4.1   Long Put

Buying put options is a fantastic way to profit from a downturning market without shorting stock. Even though both methods will make money if the market sells off, buying put options can do this with limited risk.

Put Buying versus Short Selling   Compared to short selling the stock, it is more convenient to bet against a stock by purchasing put options, as the investor does not have to borrow the stock to short. Additionally, the risk is capped to the premium paid for the put options as opposed to unlimited risk when short selling the underlying stock outright.

However, put options have a limited lifespan. If the underlying stock price does not move below the strike price before the option expiration date, the put option will expire worthless. (See Figure 4.1.)

Example   Suppose the stock of XYZ Company is trading at $40. A put option contract with a strike price of $40 expiring in a month's time is being priced at $2. You believe that XYZ stock will fall sharply in the coming weeks, so you paid $200 to purchase a single $40 XYZ put option covering 100 shares.

Say you were proven right and the price of XYZ stock crashes to $30 at option expiration date. With the underlying stock price now at $30, your put option will now be in the money with an intrinsic value of $1,000, and you can sell it for that much. Since you had paid $200 to purchase the put option, your net profit for the entire trade is therefore $800.

However, if you were wrong in your assessment and the stock price had instead rallied to $50, your put option will expire worthless, and your total loss will be the $200 that you paid to purchase the option.

Unlimited Potential   Since stock price in theory can reach zero at expiration date, the maximum profit possible when using the long put strategy is only limited to the striking price of the purchased put less the price paid for the option.

The formula for calculating profit is given next:

$$\text{Maximum profit} = \text{unlimited}$$

$$\text{Profit achieved when price of underlying} = 0$$

$$\text{Profit} = \text{strike price of long put} - \text{premium paid}$$

Limited Risk   Risk for implementing the long put strategy is limited to the price paid for the put option, no matter how high the stock price is trading on expiration date.

The formula for calculating maximum loss is given next:

$$\text{Max loss} = \text{premium paid} + \text{commissions paid}$$

$$\text{Max loss occurs when price of underlying} \geq \text{strike price of long put}$$

Breakeven Point(s)   The underlier price at which breakeven is achieved for the long put position can be calculated using the following formula:

$$\text{Breakeven point} = \text{strike price of long put} - \text{premium paid}$$

Summary   Buying put to profit in a bear situation is the simplest of options strategies but effective when timed properly. Keep in mind that going long on out-of-the-money puts may be cheaper, but the put options have a higher risk of expiring worthless. Also, in-the-money puts are more expensive than out-of-the-money puts, but the amount paid for the time value of the option is also lower.

Short In-the-Money Call

Short Call Composition

Sell 1 ITM Call

When to use: When you are bearish on market direction and also bearish on market volatility.

The in-the-money naked call strategy involves writing deep-in-the-money call options without owning the underlying stock. It is an alternative to shorting the stock and is employed when one is bearish to very bearish on the underlying.

A short is also known as a naked call. Naked calls are considered very risky positions because your risk is unlimited. (See Figure 4.2.)

Example   The stock XYZ is currently trading at $48. An options trader decides to writes a JUL 40 in-the-money call for $10. So, he or she receives $1,000 for writing the call option.

On expiration date, the stock had rallied to $68. Since the striking price of $40 for the call option is lower than the current trading price, the call is assigned, and the writer buys the shares for $6,800 and sells them to the options holder at $4,000, resulting in a loss of $2,800. However, since he or she received $1,000 earlier on, his or her net loss comes to $1,800.

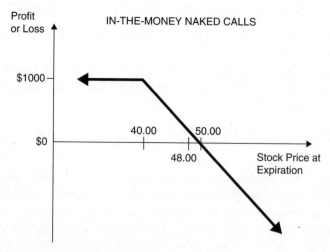

Figure 4.2 In-the-Money Naked Calls

If the stock price drops moderately to $45, the call writer can realize a profit from the loss in premium value of the call option sold. Since the striking price of $40 for the call option is lower than the current trading price, the call is assigned, and the writer buys the shares for $4,500 and sells them to the options holder at $4,000, resulting in a loss of $500. Yet, as he or she had received $1,000 for the sale of the call earlier, his or her profit for the trade is $500.

However, what happens should the stock price go down 20 points to $28 instead?

At $28, the call expires worthless, and the writer of the naked call keeps the full $1,000 in premiums received as profit.

From the profit graph shown in Figure 4.2, we can see that the breakeven is at $50 (call strike + premium). So long as the stock price remains at $50 or below, the naked call writer will not suffer any loss.

Limited Profit Potential   The main objective of writing deep-in-the-money naked calls is to collect the premiums when the call options drop in value or expire worthless as the underlying stock price declines. Profit is limited to the premium collected for writing the call options.

The formula for calculating maximum profit is given next:

$$\text{Max profit} = \text{premium received} - \text{commissions paid}$$

$$\text{Max profit achieved when price of underlying} \\ \leq \text{strike price of short call}$$

Unlimited Loss Potential   If the stock price goes up dramatically at expiration, the call writer will be required to satisfy the options requirements to sell the obligated stock to the options holder at the lower-strike price by buying the stock from the open market at higher market price. Since there is no limit to how high the stock price can be at expiration, potential losses for writing in-the-money naked calls is therefore theoretically unlimited.

The formula for calculating loss is given next:

$$\text{Maximum loss} = \text{unlimited}$$

$$\text{Loss occurs when price of underlying} \\ > \text{strike price of short call} + \text{net premium received}$$

$$\text{Loss} = \text{price of underlying} - \text{strike price of short call}$$
$$- \text{max profit} + \text{commissions paid}$$

Breakeven Point(s)   The underlier price at which breakeven is achieved for the naked call position can be calculated using the following formula:

$$\text{Breakeven point} = \text{strike price of short call} + \text{premium received}$$

Summary   This is a great bearish income strategy. Since the main objective of writing naked calls is to collect the premiums when the options expire worthless, the investor can write an out-of-the-money naked call every month. Also, if the stock price stays flat or drops, they just keep pocketing the premiums and repeating the process as long as the perceived market condition remains unchanged.

Put Backspread

Put Backspread Composition
Sell 1 ITM Put
Buy 2 OTM Puts

When to use: When you are bearish on market direction and bullish on volatility.

This strategy could also be referred to as a short put backspread; however, I will refer to this strategy simply as a put backspread.

A put backspread should be done as a credit. This means that after you buy two OTM puts and sell one ITM put, the net effect should be a credit to you. That is, you should receive money for this spread, as you are short more than you are long.

Put backspreads are a great strategy if you are bullish and bearish at the same time. They do, however, have a bias to the downside. As you can see, if the market sells off, you make unlimited profits below the breakeven point. If, however, you are wrong about the direction and the market stages a rally instead, you still win—though your profits are limited. (See Figure 4.3.)

Example   Suppose XYZ stock is trading at $48 in June. An options trader executes a 2:1 put backspread by selling a JUL 50 put for $400

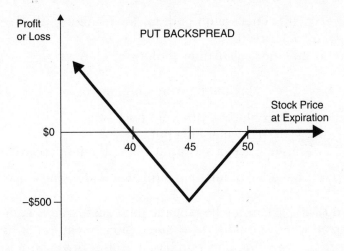

Figure 4.3 Put Backspread

and buying two JUL 45 puts for $200 each. The net debit/credit taken to enter the trade is zero.

On expiration in July, if XYZ stock is trading at $45, both the JUL 45 puts expire worthless, while the short JUL 50 put expires in the money, with $500 in intrinsic value. Buying back this put to close the position will result in the maximum loss of $500 for the options trader.

If XYZ stock drops to $40 on expiration in July, all the options will expire in the money. The short JUL 50 put is worth $1,000 and needs to be bought back to close the position. Since the two JUL 45 puts bought are now worth $500 each, their combined value of $1,000 is just enough to offset the losses from the written put. Therefore, he or she achieves breakeven at $40.

Below $40, though, there will be no limit to the gains possible. For example, at $30, each long JUL 45 put will be worth $1,500, while his or her single short JUL 50 put is only worth $2,000, resulting in a profit of $1,000.

If the stock price had rallied to $50 or higher at expiration, all the options involved will expire worthless. Since the net debit to put on this trade is zero, there is no resulting loss.

Unlimited Profit Potential This strategy profits when the stock price makes a strong move to the downside beyond the lower breakeven point. There is no limit to the maximum possible profit for the put backspread.

The formula for calculating profit is given next:

$$\text{Maximum profit} = \text{unlimited}$$

Profit achieved when price of underlying
$< 2 \times$ strike price of long put
$-$ strike price of short put $+$ net premium received

Profit $=$ strike price of long put $-$ price of underlying $-$ max loss

Limited Risk   Maximum loss for the put backspread is limited and is incurred when the underlying stock price at expiration is at the strike price of the long puts purchased. At this price, both the long puts expire worthless, while the short put expires in the money. Maximum loss is equal to the intrinsic value of the short put plus or minus any debit or credit taken when putting on the spread.

The formula for calculating maximum loss is given next:

$$\text{Max loss} = \text{strike price of short put} - \text{strike price of long put}$$
$$- \text{net premium received} + \text{commissions paid}$$

Max loss occurs when price of underlying $=$ strike price of long put

Breakeven Point(s)   There are two breakeven points for the put backspread position. The breakeven points can be calculated using the following formula:

$$\text{Upper breakeven point} = \text{strike price of short put}$$

$$\text{Lower breakeven point} = \text{strike price of long put}$$
$$- \text{points of maximum loss}$$

Call Bear Spread

Call Bear Spread Composition
Buy 1 OTM Call
Sell 1 ITM Call

When to use: When you are mildly bearish on market direction and bullish on volatility.

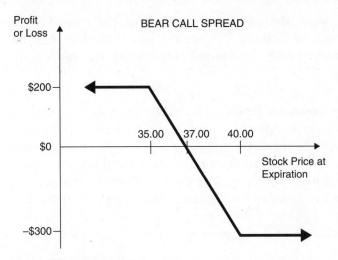

Figure 4.4 Bear Call Spread

A call bear spread is usually a credit spread. A credit spread is where the net cost of the position results in you receiving money up front for the trade. That is, you sell one call option (receive $5) and buy one call option (pay $4). The net effect is a credit of $1.

This type of spread is used when you are mildly bearish on market direction. This is the same idea as the call bull spread but reversed; that is, you think the market will go down, but you also think that the cost of a short stock or long put is too expensive. (See Figure 4.4.)

Example Suppose XYZ stock is trading at $37 in June. An options trader bearish on XYZ decides to enter a bear call spread position by buying a JUL 40 call for $100 and selling a JUL 35 call for $300 at the same time, giving him or her a net $200 credit for entering this trade.

The price of XYZ stock subsequently drops to $34 at expiration. As both options expire worthless, the options trader gets to keep the entire credit of $200 as profit.

If the stock had rallied to $42 instead, both calls will expire in the money, with the JUL 40 call bought having $200 in intrinsic value and the JUL 35 call sold having $700 in intrinsic value. The spread would then have a net value of $500 (the difference in strike prices). Since the trader has to buy back the spread for $500, this means that he or she will have a net loss of $300 after deducting the $200 credit he or she earned when he or she put on the spread position.

Limited Downside Profit   The maximum gain attainable using the bear call spread options strategy is the credit received upon entering the trade. To reach the maximum profit, the stock price needs to close below the strike price of the lower-striking call sold at expiration date where both options would expire worthless.

The formula for calculating maximum profit is given next:

$$\text{Max profit} = \text{net premium received} - \text{commissions paid}$$

$$\text{Max profit achieved when price of underlying} \leq \text{strike price of short call}$$

Limited Upside Risk   If the stock price rises above the strike price of the higher-strike call at the expiration date, then the bear call spread strategy suffers a maximum loss equal to the difference in strike price between the two options minus the original credit taken in when entering the position.

The formula for calculating maximum loss is given next:

$$\text{Max loss} = \text{strike price of long call} - \text{strike price of short call} - \text{net premium received} + \text{commissions paid}$$

Max loss occurs when price of underlying $\geq$ strike price of long call

Breakeven Point(s)   The underlier price at which breakeven is achieved for the bear call spread position can be calculated using the following formula:

$$\text{Breakeven point} = \text{strike price of short call} + \text{net premium received}$$

Summary   One can enter a more aggressive bear spread position by widening the difference between the strike prices of the two call options. However, this will also mean that the stock price must move downward by a greater degree for the trader to realize the maximum profit.

Put Bear Spread

Put Bear Spread Composition

Buy 1 ITM Put

Sell 1 OTM Put

When to use: When you are bearish on market direction and bullish on volatility.

A put bear spread has the same payoff as the call bear spread, as both strategies hope for a decrease in market prices. The choice as to which spread to use, however, comes down to risk/reward.

By shorting the out-of-the-money put, the options trader reduces the cost of establishing the bearish position but forgoes the chance of making a large profit in the event that the underlying asset price plummets. The bear put spread options strategy is also known as the bear put debit spread, as a debit is taken upon entering the trade.

A good tip is to compare the market prices of both spreads to determine which has the better payoff for you. (See Figure 4.5.)

Example   Suppose XYZ stock is trading at $38 in June. An options trader bearish on XYZ decides to enter a bear put spread position by buying a JUL 40 put for $300 and selling a JUL 35 put for $100 at the same time, resulting in a net debit of $200 for entering this position.

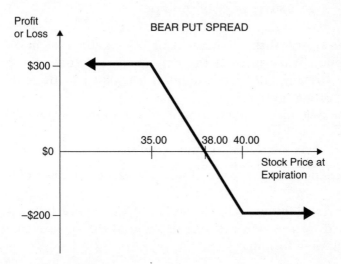

Figure 4.5 Bear Put Spread

The price of XYZ stock subsequently drops to $34 at expiration. Both puts expire in the money, with the JUL 40 call bought having $600 in intrinsic value and the JUL 35 call sold having $100 in intrinsic value. The spread would then have a net value of $5 (the difference in strike prices). Deducting the debit taken when he or she placed the trade, his or her net profit is $300. This is also his or her maximum possible profit.

If the stock had rallied to $42 instead, both options expire worthless, and the options trader loses the entire debit of $200 taken to enter the trade. This is also the maximum possible loss.

Limited Downside Profit   To reach maximum profit, the stock price needs to close below the strike price of the out-of-the-money puts on the expiration date. Both options expire in the money, but the higher-strike put that was purchased will have higher intrinsic value than the lower-strike put that was sold. Thus, maximum profit for the bear put spread option strategy is equal to the difference in strike prices minus the debit taken when the position was entered.

The formula for calculating maximum profit is given next:

$$\text{Max profit} = \text{strike price of long put} - \text{strike price of short put} \\ - \text{net premium paid} - \text{commissions paid}$$

$$\text{Max profit achieved when price of underlying} \\ \leq \text{strike price of short put}$$

Limited Upside Risk   If the stock price rises above the in-the-money put option strike price at the expiration date, then the bear put spread strategy suffers a maximum loss equal to the debit taken when putting on the trade.

The formula for calculating maximum loss is given next:

$$\text{Max loss} = \text{net premium paid} + \text{commissions paid}$$

$$\text{Max loss occurs when price of underlying} \geq \text{strike price of long put}$$

Breakeven Point(s)   The underlier price at which breakeven is achieved for the bear put spread position can be calculated using the following formula:

$$\text{Breakeven point} = \text{strike price of long put} - \text{net premium paid}$$

Hedging Techniques in Bear Markets

The techniques just outlined are usually used for pure speculation, as a separate investment to play volatility and augment profits in bear markets.

However, when you decide to short an underlying asset, it is wise to hedge your investment with the following strategies in order to reduce risk or increase profits.

Protective Call

Protective Call Composition

Short 100 Shares
Buy 1 ATM Call

When to use: When you own the underlying asset and are bullish on volatility.

The protective call is a hedging strategy whereby the trader, who has an existing short position in the underlying security, buys call options to guard against a rise in the price of that security.

A protective call strategy is usually employed when the trader is still bearish on the underlying but is wary of uncertainties in the near term. The call option is thus purchased to protect unrealized gains on the existing short position in the underlying. (See Figure 4.6.)

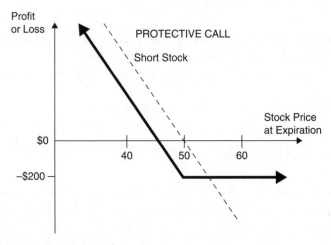

Figure 4.6 Protective Call

Example   An options trader is short 100 shares of XYZ stock trading at $50 in June. He or she implements a protective call strategy by purchasing a SEP 50 call option trading at $200 to insure his or her short position against a devastating move to the upside.

Maximum loss occurs when the stock price is $50 or higher at expiration. Even if the stock rallies to $70 on expiration, his or her max loss is capped at $200. Let's see how this works out.

At $70, his or her short stock position will suffer a loss of $2,000. However, his or her SEP 50 call will have an intrinsic value of $2,000 and can be sold for that amount. Including the initial $200 paid to buy the call option, his or her net loss will be $2,000 − $2,000 + $200 = $200.

Unlimited Profit Potential   The protective call is also known as a synthetic long put, as its risk/reward profile is the same as that of the long put. Like the long put strategy, there is no limit to the maximum profit attainable using this strategy.

The formula for calculating profit is given next:

$$\text{Maximum profit} = \text{unlimited}$$

$$\text{Profit achieved when price of underlying} \\ < \text{sale price of underlying} - \text{premium paid}$$

$$\text{Profit} = \text{sale price of underlying} - \text{price of underlying} \\ - \text{premium paid}$$

Limited Risk   Maximum loss for this strategy is limited and is equal to the premium paid for buying the call option.

The formula for calculating maximum loss is given next:

$$\text{Max loss} = \text{premium paid} + \text{call strike price} \\ - \text{sale price of underlying} + \text{commissions paid}$$

$$\text{Max loss occurs when price of underlying} \leq \text{strike price of long put}$$

Breakeven Point(s)   The underlier price at which breakeven is achieved for the protective call position can be calculated using the following formula:

$$\text{Breakeven point} = \text{sale price of underlying} + \text{premium paid}$$

Covered Put

Covered Put Composition

Short 100 Shares
Sell 1 ATM Put

When to use: To increase your profits when shorting shares or to protect your short share position from a slight rise in price.

The covered put, also known as selling covered puts, is a lesser-known variant of the popular covered call option strategy. In a covered call, you buy shares and sell call options against them in order to profit from a stagnant or bullish move, while in a covered put, you short shares and then sell put options against them in order to profit from a stagnant or bearish move.

Selling put options in this case is considered "covered" due to the short shares. If the short put options are assigned, shares will be delivered, which will cover the short share position.

The covered put is not a common strategy option traders use when speculating a stagnant or bearish move in the underlying stock, because a covered put has a limited profit potential along with an unlimited loss potential. Couple this with the fact that most shares rise over time, and the covered put is always exposed to the danger of unlimited loss. When speculating a quick bearish move on the underlying stock, most option traders prefer to use other complex bearish strategies that profit from both a bearish and stagnant move on the underlying move like the bear ratio spread.

A covered put is most commonly used by share traders to increase the profits from shorting shares and also to protect a short share position against a slight rise in price. In the first scenario, if the underlying stock should drop to the strike price of the put options sold, one would make the drop in price on the underlying stock plus the premium on the put options sold as profit. In this case, the premium on the put options sold serves as additional profits. In the second scenario, the premium on the put options serves to offset the loss on the short shares should the underlying stock rise. (See Figure 4.7.)

Example   Suppose XYZ stock is trading at $45 in June. An options trader writes a covered put by selling a JUL 45 put for $200 while

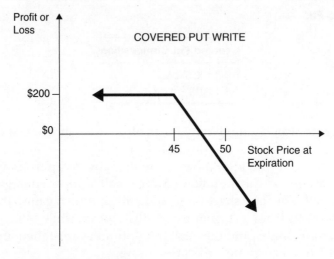

Figure 4.7   Covered Put Write

shorting 100 shares of XYZ stock. The net credit taken to enter the position is $200, which is also his or her maximum possible profit.

On expiration in July, XYZ stock is still trading at $45. The JUL 45 put expires worthless, while the trader covers his or her short position with no loss. In the end, he or she gets to keep the entire credit taken as profit.

If instead, XYZ stock drops to $40 on expiration, the short put will expire in the money and is worth $500, but this loss is offset by the $500 gain in the short stock position. Thus, the profit is still the initial credit of $200 taken on entering the trade.

However, should the stock rally to $55 on expiration, a significant loss results. At this price, the short stock position taken when XYZ stock was trading at $45 suffers a $1,000 loss. Subtracting the initial credit of $200 taken, the resulting loss is $800.

Limited Profits with No Downside Risk   Profit for the covered put option strategy is limited, and maximum gain is equal to the premiums received for the options sold.

The formula for calculating maximum profit is given next:

$$\text{Max profit} = \text{premium received} - \text{commissions paid}$$

Max profit achieved when price of underlying
$\leq$ strike price of short put

Unlimited Upside Risk   As the writer is short on the stock, he or she is subjected to much risk if the price of the underlying stock rises dramatically. In theory, maximum loss for the covered put options strategy is unlimited, since there is no limit to how high the stock price can be at expiration. If applicable, the covered put writer will also have to pay out any dividends.

The formula for calculating loss is given next:

$$\text{Maximum loss} = \text{unlimited}$$

$$\text{Loss occurs when price of underlying} \geq \text{sale price of underlying} + \text{premium received}$$

$$\text{Loss} = \text{price of underlying} - \text{sale price of underlying} - \text{premium received} + \text{commissions paid}$$

Breakeven Point(s)   The underlier price at which breakeven is achieved for the covered put position can be calculated using the following formula:

$$\text{Breakeven point} = \text{sale price of underlying} + \text{premium received}$$

Conclusion

In this chapter, we covered a wide range of techniques that any investor can use to profit when in a bearish environment. Keep in mind that bear markets are much more volatile than bull markets. Bull markets tend to be more slow and steady, whereas bear markets are full of panic, which causes extreme volatility.

Make sure when you implement the strategies that are outlined in this chapter that you pay special attention to implied and historical volatility when choosing which options to buy and sell.

CHAPTER 5

Slaughtering the Pigs

This chapter pays special attention to volatility and how to make money when you expect the market to trend sideways (volatility bear) or how to profit when you expect a large move in the underlying asset, but you aren't sure in what direction (volatility bull).

The strategies in this chapter are by far the most complex. They give you great ways to make money when you do know which way the market is going to go; these techniques are often called neutral trading strategies, or nondirectional strategies.

They are so named because the potential to profit does not depend on whether the underlying stock price will go upward or downward. Rather, the correct neutral strategy to employ depends on the expected volatility of the underlying stock price.

When a trader is bullish on volatility, he or she can employ neutral trading strategies that profit when the underlying stock price experience has big moves upward or downward, including the long straddle, long strangle, short condors, and short butterflies.

On the other hand, when a trader is bearish on volatility, he or she can use neutral trading strategies that profit when the underlying stock price experience has little or no movement, including the short straddle, short strangle, ratio spreads, long condors, and long butterflies.

While these trading techniques might be more complicated, they are far more exciting and can make you a lot of money without the stress of having to guess which way the market is going to move.

Just remember to take both implied and historical volatility into account when buying and selling options. You want to sell options when they are overpriced (implied volatility is higher than historical volatility), and you want to buy options when they are trading at a discount (implied volatility is lower than historical volatility). As I said earlier, there are plenty of programs available that will calculate both historical and implied volatility for you—I prefer OptionsVue.

Minding the Spread Width

The spread width (difference between the strike prices of the long and short side of two calls or two puts) establishes how much money is at risk. Sadly, this point is ignored by too many investors who assume the position is so safe (because the options sold are far OTM) that it doesn't matter which option is bought, as long as some option is purchased. When the spread is narrow, the premium collected, the profit potential, and the maximum loss (the spread × 100, minus the cash premium collected) are all reduced. When the spread is wide, more cash is collected, but the potential loss is higher. It is important to remember this when trading neutral strategies.

Techniques When Bullish on Volatility

The strategies outlined in this section are to be used when you expect volatility to increase and you are anticipating a large move in the underlying asset, but you don't know in which direction.

Long Straddle

Long Straddle Construction
Buy 1 ATM Call
Buy 1 ATM Put

When to use: When you are bullish on volatility but are unsure of market direction.

A long straddle is an excellent strategy to use when you think the market is going to move, but you don't know in which way. A long straddle is like placing an each-way bet on price action: You make money if the market goes up or down.

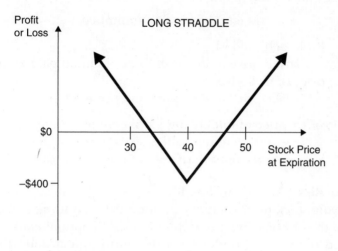

Figure 5.1   Long Straddle

But the market must move enough in either direction to cover the cost of buying both options.

Buying straddles is best when implied volatility is low or when you expect the market to make a substantial move before the expiration date—for example, before an earnings announcement. (See Figure 5.1.)

Example   Suppose XYZ stock is trading at $40 in June. An options trader enters a long straddle by buying a JUL 40 put for $200 and a JUL 40 call for $200. The net debit taken to enter the trade is $400, which is also his or her maximum possible loss.

If XYZ stock is trading at $50 on expiration in July, the JUL 40 put will expire worthless, but the JUL 40 call will expire in the money and will have an intrinsic value of $1,000. Subtracting the initial debit of $400, the long straddle trader's profit comes to $600.

On expiration in July, if XYZ stock is still trading at $40, both the JUL 40 put and the JUL 40 call expire worthless, and the long straddle trader suffers a maximum loss, which is equal to the initial debit of $400 taken to enter the trade.

Unlimited Profit Potential   By having long positions in both call and put options, straddles can achieve large profits, no matter which way the underlying stock price heads, provided the move is strong enough.

The formula for calculating profit is given next:

Maximum profit = unlimited

Profit achieved when price of underlying
> strike price of long call + net premium paid *or*
price of underlying
< strike price of long put – net premium paid

Profit = price of underlying – strike price of long call
– net premium paid *or* strike price of long put
– price of underlying – net premium paid

Limited Risk   Maximum loss for long straddles occurs when the underlying stock price on the expiration date is trading at the strike price of the options bought. At this price, both options expire worthless, and the options trader loses the entire initial debit taken to enter the trade.

The formula for calculating maximum loss is given next:

Max loss = net premium paid + commissions paid

Max loss occurs when price of underlying
= strike price of long call/put

Breakeven Point(s)   There are two breakeven points for the long straddle position. The breakeven points can be calculated using the following formula:

Upper breakeven point = strike price of long call
+ net premium paid

Lower breakeven point = strike price of long put
– net premium paid

Summary   There are two modifications of the straddle strategy, the strap and the strip, which can be implemented to introduce a bullish or bearish bias to the risk/reward curve, respectively.

Strap Straddle

Strap Straddle Construction
Buy 2 ATM Calls
Buy 1 ATM Put

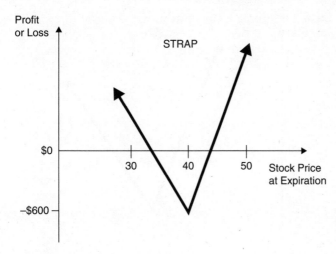

Figure 5.2   Strap Saddle

When to use: When you are bullish on volatility but are unsure of market direction; however, you are leaning toward the upside.

To implement a more bullish bias to a straddle, just double the amount of ATM calls you buy in relation to the puts. The profit/loss chart is shown in Figure 5.2.

Example   Suppose XYZ stock is trading at $40 in June. An options trader implements a strap by buying two JUL 40 calls for $400 and a JUL 40 put for $200. The net debit taken to enter the trade is $600, which is also his or her maximum possible loss.

If XYZ stock price plunges to $30 on expiration in July, the JUL 40 calls will expire worthless, but the JUL 40 put will expire in the money and will possess intrinsic value of $1,000. Subtracting the initial debit of $600, the strap's profit comes to $400.

If XYZ stock is trading at $50 on expiration in July, the JUL 40 put will expire worthless, but the two JUL 40 calls will expire in the money and will have intrinsic values of $1,000 each. Subtracting the initial debit of $600, the strap's profit comes to $1,400.

On expiration in July, if XYZ stock is still trading at $40, both the JUL 40 put and the JUL 40 calls expire worthless, and the strap suffers its maximum loss, which is equal to the initial debit of $600 taken to enter the trade.

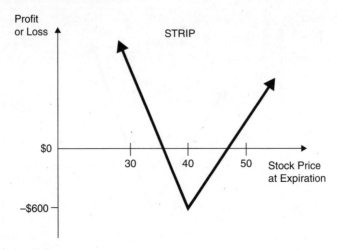

Figure 5.3   Strip Saddle

Strip Straddle

Strip Straddle Construction

Buy 1 ATM Call
Buy 2 ATM Puts

When to use: When you are bullish on volatility but are unsure of market direction; however, you are leaning toward the downside.

To implement a more bearish bias to a straddle, double the amount of ATM puts you buy in relation to the calls; this is called a strip spread. Figure 5.3 shows the profit/loss chart.

Example   Suppose XYZ stock is trading at $40 in June. An options trader implements a strip by buying two JUL 40 puts for $400 and a JUL 40 call for $200. The net debit taken to enter the trade is $600, which is also his or her maximum possible loss.

If XYZ stock is trading at $50 on expiration in July, the JUL 40 puts will expire worthless, but the JUL 40 call will expire in the money and will have an intrinsic value of $1,000. Subtracting the initial debit of $600, the strip's profit comes to $400.

If XYZ stock price plunges to $30 on expiration in July, the JUL 40 call will expire worthless, but the two JUL 40 puts will expire in the money and will possess intrinsic values of $1,000 each. Subtracting the initial debit of $600, the strip's profit comes to $1,400.

On expiration in July, if XYZ stock is still trading at $40, both the JUL 40 puts and the JUL 40 call expire worthless, and the strip suffers its maximum loss, which is equal to the initial debit of $600 taken to enter the trade.

Summary The straddle is the most basic of the high-volatility strategies but is very effective—especially when you are able to purchase options at a discount (lower implied volatility in respect to historical volatility).

Long Strangle

Long Strangle Composition

Buy 1 OTM Call
Buy 1 OTM Put

When to use: When you are bullish on volatility but are unsure of market direction.

A long strangle is similar to a straddle, except the strike prices are further apart, which lowers the cost of putting on the spread and widens the gap needed for the market to rise/fall beyond in order to be profitable.

Like long straddles, buying strangles is best when implied volatility is low or when you expect a large movement of market price in either direction. (See Figure 5.4.)

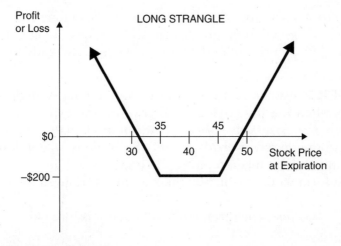

Figure 5.4 Long Strangle

Example   Suppose XYZ stock is trading at $40 in June. An options trader executes a long strangle by buying a JUL 35 put for $100 and a JUL 45 call for $100. The net debit taken to enter the trade is $200, which is also his or her maximum possible loss.

If XYZ stock rallies and is trading at $50 on expiration in July, the JUL 35 put will expire worthless, but the JUL 45 call will expire in the money and will have an intrinsic value of $500. Subtracting the initial debit of $200, the options trader's profit comes to $300.

On expiration in July, if XYZ stock is still trading at $40, both the JUL 35 put and the JUL 45 call expire worthless, and the options trader suffers a maximum loss, which is equal to the initial debit of $200 taken to enter the trade.

Unlimited Profit Potential   Large gains are attainable using the long strangle option strategy when the underlying stock price makes a very strong move either upward or downward at expiration.

The formula for calculating profit is given next:

$$\text{Maximum profit} = \text{unlimited}$$

Profit achieved when price of underlying
> strike price of long call + net premium paid *or*
price of underlying
< strike price of long put − net premium paid

Profit = price of underlying − strike price of long call
− net premium paid *or* strike price of long put
− price of underlying − net premium paid

Limited Risk   Maximum loss is hit using the long strangle option strategy when the underlying stock price on the expiration date is trading between the strike prices of the options bought. At this price, both options expire worthless, and the options trader loses the entire initial debit taken to enter the trade.

The formula for calculating maximum loss is given next:

$$\text{Max loss} = \text{net premium paid} + \text{commissions paid}$$

Max loss occurs when price of underlying is between strike price of long call and strike price of long put.

Breakeven Point(s)   There are two breakeven points for the long strangle position. The breakeven points can be calculated using the following formulas:

Upper breakeven point = strike price of long call
+ net premium paid

Lower breakeven point = strike price of long put
− net premium paid

Short Call Ladder

Short Call Ladder Composition
Sell 1 ITM Call
Buy 1 ATM Call
Buy 1 OTM Call

When to use: When you are bullish on volatility.

The short call ladder, or bear call ladder, is an unlimited-profit and limited-risk strategy in options trading that is employed when the options trader thinks that the underlying security will experience significant volatility in the near term.

To set up the short call ladder, the options trader sells an in-the-money call, purchases an at-the-money call, and purchases another higher-strike out-of-the-money call of the same underlying security and expiration date. (See Figure 5.5.)

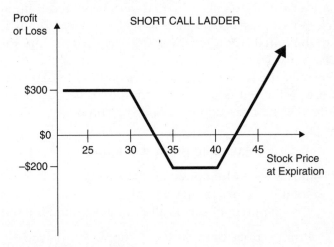

Figure 5.5 Short Call Ladder

Example   Suppose XYZ stock is trading at $35 in June. An options trader executes a short call ladder strategy by selling a JUL 30 call for $600 and buying a JUL 35 call for $200 and a JUL 40 call for $100. The net credit received for entering this trade is $300.

In the event that XYZ stock rallies and is trading at $50 on expiration in July, all the call options will expire in the money. The long JUL 35 call will expire with $1,500 in intrinsic value, while the long JUL 40 call will expire with $1,000 in intrinsic value.

Buying back the short JUL 30 call will only cost the options trader $2,000. Therefore, selling the long calls and buying back the short call will leave the trader with a $500 gain. Together with the initial credit of $300, his or her total profit comes to $800. This profit could have been even higher if the stock had rallied beyond $50.

However, if the stock price had dropped to $30 instead, all the calls would expire worthless, and his or her profit would only be the initial credit of $300 received.

On the other hand, let's say XYZ stock remains at $35 on expiration date. At this price, only the short JUL 30 call will expire in the money, with an intrinsic value of $500. Taking into account the initial credit of $300, buying back this call to close the position will leave the trader with a $200 loss; this is also his or her maximum possible loss.

Limited Downside, Unlimited Upside Profit Potential   The maximum gain for the short call ladder strategy is limited if the underlying stock price goes down. In this scenario, maximum profit is limited to the initial credit received, since all the long and short calls will expire worthless.

However, if the underlying stock price rallies explosively, potential profit is unlimited due to the extra long call.

The formula for calculating profit is given next:

$$\text{Maximum profit} = \text{unlimited}$$

Profit achieved when price of underlying
  > total strike prices of long calls
      − strike price of short call + net premium received

Profit = price of underlying − upper breakeven

Limited Risk   Losses are limited when employing the short call ladder strategy, and maximum loss occurs when the stock price is between the strike prices of the two long calls on expiration date. At this price, the higher-striking long call expires worthless, while the lower-striking long call is worth much less than the short call, thus resulting in a loss.

The formula for calculating maximum loss is given next:

$$
\begin{aligned}
\text{Max loss} = \ & \text{strike price of lower-strike long call} \\
& - \text{strike price of short call} \\
& - \text{net premium received} \\
& + \text{commissions paid}
\end{aligned}
$$

Max loss occurs when price of underlying is between the strike prices of the two long calls.

Breakeven Point(s)   There are two breakeven points for the short call ladder position. The breakeven points can be calculated using the following formulae:

$$
\begin{aligned}
\text{Upper breakeven point} = \ & \text{total strike prices of long calls} \\
& - \text{strike price of short call} \\
& + \text{net premium received}
\end{aligned}
$$

$$
\begin{aligned}
\text{Lower breakeven point} = \ & \text{strike price of short call} \\
& - \text{net premium received}
\end{aligned}
$$

Short Put Ladder

Short Put Ladder Composition
Sell 1 ITM Put
Buy 1 ATM Put
Buy 1 OTM Put

When to use: When you are bullish on volatility.

The short put ladder, or bull put ladder, is an unlimited-profit, limited-risk strategy in options trading that is employed when the options trader thinks that the underlying security will experience significant volatility in the near term.

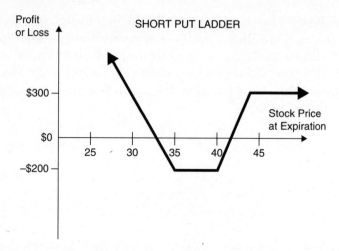

Figure 5.6   Short Put Ladder

To set up the short put ladder, the options trader sells an in-the-money put, buys an at-the-money put, and buys another lower-strike out-of-the-money put of the same underlying security and expiration date. (See Figure 5.6.)

Example   Suppose XYZ stock is trading at $40 in June. An options trader executes a short put ladder strategy by selling a JUL 45 put for $600 and buying a JUL 40 put for $200 and a JUL 35 put for $100. The net credit received for entering this trade is $300.

Let's say XYZ stock remains at $40 on expiration date. At this price, only the short JUL 45 put will expire in the money, with an intrinsic value of $500. Taking into account the initial credit of $300, buying back this put to close the position will leave the trader with a $200 loss, which is also his or her maximum possible loss.

In the event that XYZ stock rallies and is trading at $45 on expiration in July, all the puts will expire worthless, and the trader's profit will be the initial $300 credit received when entering the trade.

However, if the stock price had dropped to $25 instead, all the put options would expire in the money. The long JUL 40 put would expire with $1,500 in intrinsic value, while the long JUL 35 put would expire with $1,000 in intrinsic value. Buying back the short JUL 45 put would only cost the options trader $2,000, so he or she would still have a gain of $500 when closing the position. Together with the initial credit of $300, his or her total profit comes to $800. This profit could have been greater if the stock had dived below $25.

Unlimited Downside, Limited Upside Profit Potential   Maximum gain is limited to the initial credit received if the stock price rallies above the upper breakeven point, but large unlimited profit can be achieved should the stock price make a dramatic move to the downside below the lower breakeven point.
   The formula for calculating profit is given next:

$$\text{Maximum profit} = \text{unlimited}$$

Profit achieved when price of underlying
   < total strike prices of long puts
      − strike price of short put + net premium received

$$\text{Profit} = \text{lower breakeven} - \text{price of underlying}$$

Limited Risk   Maximum loss for the short put ladder strategy is limited and occurs when the underlying stock price on expiration date is trading between the strike prices of the put options bought. At this price, while both the short put and the higher-strike long put expire in the money, the short put is worth more than the long put, resulting in a loss.
   The formula for calculating maximum loss is given next:

Max loss = strike price of short put
            − strike price of higher-strike long put
            − net premium received + commissions paid

Max loss occurs when price of underlying is between the strike prices of the two long puts.

Breakeven Point(s)   There are two breakeven points for the short put ladder position. The breakeven points can be calculated using the following formula:

Upper breakeven point = strike price of short put
                           − net premium received

Lower breakeven point = total strike prices of long puts
− strike price of short put
+ net premium received

Short Condor

Short Condor Construction
Buy 1 ITM Call
Sell 1 ITM Call (Lower Strike)
Buy 1 OTM Call
Sell 1 OTM Call (Higher Strike)

When to use: When you are bullish on volatility, and you are unsure of which direction the market will move.

The short condor is a neutral strategy and is a limited-risk/limited-profit trading strategy that is structured to earn a profit when the underlying stock is perceived to be making a sharp move in either direction.

Using calls, the options trader can set up a short condor by combining a bear call spread and a bull call spread. The trader enters a short call condor by buying a lower-strike in-the-money call, selling an even lower-striking in-the-money call, buying a higher-

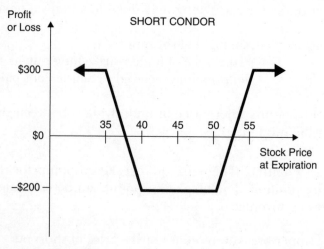

Figure 5.7   Short Condor

strike out-of-the-money call, and selling another even higher-striking out-of-the-money call. A total of four legs are involved in this trading strategy, and a net credit is received on entering the trade.

Example   Suppose XYZ stock is trading at $45 in June. An options trader executes a short condor by selling a JUL 35 call for $1,100, buying a JUL 40 call for $700, buying another JUL 50 call for $200, and selling another JUL 55 call for $100. A net credit of $300 is received on entering the trade.

To further see why $300 is the maximum possible profit, let's examine what happens when the stock price falls to $35 or rises to $55 on expiration.

At $35, all the options expire worthless, so the initial credit taken of $300 is his or her maximum profit.

At $55, the short JUL 55 call expires worthless, while the profit from the long JUL 40 call (worth $1,500) and the long JUL 50 call (worth $500) is used to offset the short JUL 35 call worth $2,000. Thus, the short condor trader still earns the maximum profit, which is equal to the $300 initial credit taken when entering the trade.

On the flip side, if XYZ stock is still trading at $45 on expiration in July, only the JUL 35 call and the JUL 40 call expire in the money. With his or her long JUL 40 call worth $500 and the initial credit of $300 received to offset the short JUL 35 call valued at $1,000, there is still a net loss of $200. This is the maximum possible loss and is suffered when the underlying stock price at expiration is anywhere between $40 and $50.

Limited Profit Potential   The maximum possible profit for a short condor is equal to the initial credit received upon entering the trade. It happens when the underlying stock price on expiration date is at or below the lowest strike price and also occurs when the stock price is at or above the highest strike price of all the options involved.

The formula for calculating maximum profit is given next:

Max profit = net premium received − commissions paid

Max profit achieved when price of underlying
≤ strike price of lower-strike short call *or* price of underlying
≥ strike price of higher-strike short call

Limited Risk   Maximum loss is suffered when the underlying stock price falls between the two middle strikes at expiration. It can be derived that the maximum loss is equal to the difference in strike prices of the two lower-striking calls less the initial credit taken to enter the trade.

The formula for calculating maximum loss is given next:

$$\text{Max loss} = \text{strike price of lower-strike long call}$$
$$- \text{strike price of lower-strike short call}$$
$$- \text{net premium received} + \text{commissions paid}$$

Max loss occurs when price of underlying is between the strike prices of the two long calls.

Breakeven Point(s)   There are two breakeven points for the short condor position. The breakeven points can be calculated using the following formulas:

$$\text{Upper breakeven point} = \text{strike price of highest strike short call}$$
$$- \text{net premium paid}$$

$$\text{Lower breakeven point} = \text{strike price of lowest strike short call}$$
$$+ \text{net premium paid}$$

Short Call Butterfly

Short Call Butterfly Composition
Sell 1 ITM Call
Buy 2 ATM Calls
Sell 1 OTM Call

When to use: When you are neutral on market direction and bullish on volatility.

Being neutral on market direction means that you want the market to move in either direction—basically being bullish and bearish at the same time.

Short call butterflies have similar payoffs to the long straddle, in that the downside risk is limited. A short butterfly's risk is limited to the premium paid for the three options. (See Figure 5.8.)

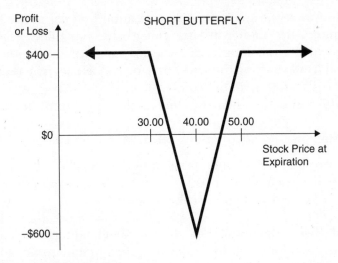

Figure 5.8 **Short Butterfly**

Example Suppose XYZ stock is trading at $40 in June. An options trader executes a short call butterfly strategy by writing a JUL 30 call for $1,100, buying two JUL 40 calls for $400 each, and writing another JUL 50 call for $100. The net credit taken to enter the position is $400, which is also his or her maximum possible profit.

On expiration in July, XYZ stock has dropped to $30. All the options expire worthless, and the short butterfly trader gets to keep the entire initial credit taken of $400 as profit. This is also the maximum profit attainable and would be obtained even if the stock had instead rallied to $50 or beyond.

On the downside, should the stock price remain at $40 at expiration, maximum loss will be incurred. At this price, all except the lower-striking call would expire worthless. The lower-striking call sold short would have a value of $1,000 and would need to be bought back. Subtracting the initial credit of $400 taken, the net loss (maximum) is equal to $600.

Limited Profit Maximum profit for the short butterfly is obtained when the underlying stock price rallies pass the higher-strike price or drops below the lower-strike price at expiration.

If the stock ends up at the lower-striking price, all the options expire worthless, and the short butterfly trader keeps the initial credit taken when entering the position.

However, if the stock price at expiration is equal to the higher-strike price, the higher-striking call expires worthless, while the "profits" of the two long calls owned is canceled out by the "loss" incurred from shorting the lower-striking call. Hence, the maximum profit is still only the initial credit taken.

The formula for calculating maximum profit is given next:

Max profit = net premium received − commissions paid

Max profit achieved when price of underlying
≤ strike price of lower-strike short call *or* price of underlying
≥ strike price of higher-strike short call

Limited Risk   Maximum loss for the short butterfly is incurred when the stock price of the underlying stock remains unchanged at expiration. At this price, only the lower-striking call that was shorted expires in the money. The trader will have to buy back the call at its intrinsic value.

The formula for calculating maximum loss is given next:

Max loss = strike price of long call
− strike price of lower-strike short call
− net premium received + commissions paid

Max loss occurs when price of underlying = strike price of long calls

Breakeven Point(s)   There are two breakeven points for the short butterfly position. The breakeven points can be calculated using the following formulas:

Upper breakeven point = strike price of highest strike short call
− net premium received

Lower breakeven point = strike price of lowest strike short call
+ net premium received

Summary   You can also construct the short put butterfly using the exact same composition—just substitute the calls with puts.

Techniques When Bearish on Volatility

The strategies outlined in this section are to be used when you expect volatility to decrease and you are anticipating the underlying asset to trend sideways for a certain time period. The simplest of these strategies is either a short straddle or strangle. These are identical to the long straddle or strangle—but you sell the options instead of buying them. The problem with the short straddle and strangle is that they have a very limited profit potential and an unlimited loss potential.

The following strategies are ways to trade bearish volatility without exposing yourself to unlimited loss risk.

Long Call Butterfly Spread

Long Call Butterfly Spread Composition
Buy 1 ITM Call
Sell 2 ATM Calls
Buy 1 OTM Call

When to use: When you are neutral on market direction and bearish on volatility.

A long butterfly is similar to a short straddle, except your losses are limited. This means that you make money when the market remains flat over the life of the options.

You might be thinking that it looks like a "short" strategy because of the similarity to the short straddle. You are right in thinking that they have similar characteristics; however, the difference between a long butterfly and a short straddle is the premium: A long butterfly will cost you money (or premium) to establish, whereas a short straddle won't cost you anything, as you receive money (premium) up front for putting on the position. (See Figure 5.9.)

Example Suppose XYZ stock is trading at $40 in June. An options trader executes a long call butterfly by purchasing a JUL 30 call for $1,100, writing two JUL 40 calls for $400 each, and purchasing another JUL 50 call for $100. The net debit taken to enter the position is $400, which is also his or her maximum possible loss.

On expiration in July, XYZ stock is still trading at $40. The JUL 40 calls and the JUL 50 call expire worthless, while the JUL 30 call still has an intrinsic value of $1,000. Subtracting the initial debit of $400, the resulting profit is $600, which is also the maximum profit attainable.

Maximum loss results when the stock is trading below $30 or above $50. At $30, all the options expire worthless. Above $50, any

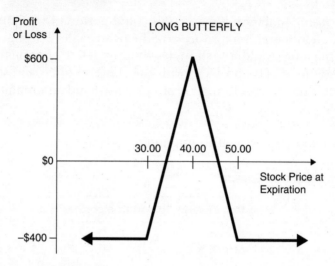

Figure 5.9 Long Butterfly

"profit" from the two long calls will be neutralized by the "loss" from the two short calls. In both situations, the butterfly trader suffers maximum loss, which is the initial debit taken to enter the trade.

Limited Profit Potential Maximum profit for the long butterfly spread is attained when the underlying stock price remains unchanged at expiration. At this price, only the lower-striking call expires in the money.

The formula for calculating maximum profit is given next:

> Max profit = strike price of short call
> − strike price of lower-strike long call
> − net premium paid − commissions paid
>
> Max profit achieved when price of underlying
> = strike price of short calls

Limited Risk Maximum loss for the long butterfly spread is limited to the initial debit taken to enter the trade plus commissions.

The formula for calculating maximum loss is given next:

> Max loss = net premium paid + commissions paid

Max loss occurs when price of underlying
  ≤ strike price of lower-strike long call *or* price of underlying
  ≥ strike price of higher-strike long call

Breakeven Point(s)   There are two breakeven points for the butterfly spread position. The breakeven points can be calculated using
the following formulas:

Upper breakeven point = strike price of higher-strike long call
                                 − net premium paid

Lower breakeven point = strike price of lower-strike long call
                                 + net premium paid

Summary   The long call butterfly is an excellent strategy in a sideways market. You can also construct the long put butterfly using the
exact same composition—just substitute the calls with puts. If you
really want to be extremely neutral, you can construct a long call
butterfly and a long put butterfly on both sides of an underlying
asset.

Iron Condor

Iron Condor Composition
Sell 1 ITM Call
Buy 1 ITM Call (Lower Strike)
Sell 1 OTM Call
Buy 1 OTM Call (Higher Strike)

When to use: When you are neutral on market direction and
bearish on volatility.

Just like a long butterfly, iron condors are used when an investor
believes that the underlying market will trade in a range (sideways)
up until the options expire.

Condors are best used when the options are close to expiration.
If the options are longer dated, then the underlying asset has more
chances to break away and trade outside of the boundary exercise
prices. A total of four legs are involved in the condor options strategy, and a net debit is required to establish the position. (See Figure
5.10.)

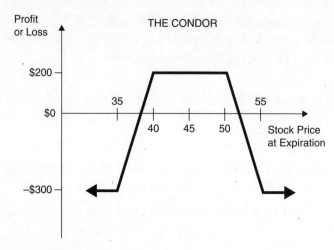

Figure 5.10   The Condor

Example   Suppose XYZ stock is trading at $45 in June. An options trader enters a condor trade by buying a JUL 35 call for $1,100, writing a JUL 40 call for $700, writing another JUL 50 call for $200, and buying another JUL 55 call for $100. The net debit required to enter the trade is $300, which is also his or her maximum possible loss.

To further see why $300 is the maximum possible loss, let's examine what happens when the stock price falls to $35 or rises to $55 on expiration.

At $35, all the options expire worthless, so the initial debit taken of $300 is his or her maximum loss.

At $55, the long JUL 55 call expires worthless, while the long JUL 35 call worth $2,000 is used to offset the loss from the short JUL 40 call (worth $1,500) and the short JUL 50 call (worth $500). Thus, the long condor trader still suffers the maximum loss, which is equal to the $300 initial debit taken when entering the trade.

If instead, on expiration in July, XYZ stock is still trading at $45, only the JUL 35 call and the JUL 40 call expire in the money. With his or her long JUL 35 call worth $1,000 to offset the short JUL 40 call valued at $500 and the initial debit of $300, his or her net profit comes to $200.

The maximum profit for the condor trade may be low in relation to other trading strategies, but it has a comparatively wider profit zone. In this example, maximum profit is achieved if the underlying stock price at expiration is anywhere between $40 and $50.

Limited Profit   Maximum profit for the long condor option strategy is achieved when the stock price falls between the two middle strikes at expiration. It can be derived that the maximum profit is equal to the difference in strike prices of the two lower-striking calls less the initial debit taken to enter the trade.

The formula for calculating maximum profit is given next:

$$\begin{aligned} \text{Max profit} = &\text{ strike price of lower-strike short call} \\ &- \text{strike price of lower-strike long call} \\ &- \text{net premium paid} - \text{commissions paid} \end{aligned}$$

Max profit is achieved when price of underlying is between the strike prices of the two short calls.

Limited Risk   The maximum possible loss for a long condor option strategy is equal to the initial debit taken when entering the trade. It happens when the underlying stock price on expiration date is at or below the lowest strike price and also occurs when the stock price is at or above the highest strike price of all the options involved.

The formula for calculating maximum loss is given next:

$$\text{Max loss} = \text{net premium paid} + \text{commissions paid}$$

Max loss occurs when price of underlying
  $\leq$ strike price of lower-strike long call *or* price of underlying
  $\geq$ strike price of higher-strike long call

Breakeven Point(s)   There are two breakeven points for the condor position. The breakeven points can be calculated using the following formulas:

$$\begin{aligned} \text{Upper breakeven point} = &\text{ strike price of highest strike long call} \\ &- \text{net premium received} \end{aligned}$$

$$\begin{aligned} \text{Lower breakeven point} = &\text{ strike price of lowest strike long call} \\ &+ \text{net premium received} \end{aligned}$$

Call Ratio Spread

Call Ratio Spread Composition
Buy 1 ITM Call
Sell 2 OTM Calls

When to use: When you are bearish on volatility and neutral on market direction.

Even though a call ratio vertical spread is the reverse of a call backspread, it is generally not referred to as being short a call backspread, as a call ratio spread requires upfront payment and is hence a long strategy.

You will notice that it is very similar to a short strangle, except the risk is limited on the downside. This ratio spread can also be constructed using puts. The put ratio spread is similar to the call ratio spread strategy but has a slightly more bullish and less bearish risk profile. (See Figure 5.11.)

Example   Suppose XYZ stock is trading at $43 in June. An options trader executes a 2:1 ratio call spread strategy by buying a JUL 40 call for $400 and selling two JUL 45 calls for $200 each. The net debit/credit taken to enter the trade is zero.

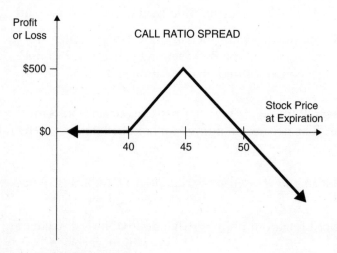

Figure 5.11   Call Ratio Spread

On expiration in July, if XYZ stock is trading at $45, both the JUL 45 calls expire worthless, while the long JUL 40 call expires in the money, with $500 in intrinsic value. Selling or exercising this long call will give the options trader his or her maximum profit of $500.

If XYZ stock rallies and is trading at $50 on expiration in July, all the options will expire in the money, but because the trader has written more calls than he or she has bought, he or she will need to buy back the written calls that have increased in value. Each JUL 45 call written is now worth $500. However, his or her long JUL 40 call is worth $1,000 and is just enough to offset the losses from the written calls. Therefore, he or she achieves breakeven at $50.

Beyond $50, though, there will be no limit to the loss possible. For example, at $60, each written JUL 45 call will be worth $1,500, while his or her single long JUL 40 call will only be worth $2,000, resulting in a loss of $1,000.

However, there is no downside risk to this trade. If the stock price had dropped to $40 or below at expiration, all the options involved would have expired worthless. Since the net debit to put on this trade is zero, there is no resulting loss.

Limited Profit Potential   Maximum gain for the call ratio spread is limited and is made when the underlying stock price at expiration is at the strike price of the options sold. At this price, both the written calls expire worthless, while the long call expires in the money.

The formula for calculating maximum profit is given next:

$$\text{Max profit} = \text{strike price of short call} - \text{strike price of long call} \\ + \text{net premium received} - \text{commissions paid}$$

$$\text{Max profit achieved when price of underlying} \\ = \text{strike price of short calls}$$

Unlimited Upside Risk   Loss occurs when the stock price makes a strong move to the upside beyond the upper breakeven point. There is no limit to the maximum possible loss when implementing the call ratio spread strategy.

The formula for calculating loss is given next:

$$\text{Maximum loss} = \text{unlimited}$$

Loss occurs when price of underlying
  > strike price of short calls + [(strike price of short call
    − strike price of long call + net premium received)/
    number of uncovered calls]

Loss = price of underlying-strike price of short calls
        − max profit + commissions paid

Little or No Downside Risk   Any risk to the downside for the call ratio spread is limited to the debit taken to put on the spread (if any). There may even be a profit if a credit is received when putting on the spread.

Breakeven Point(s)   There are two breakeven points for the ratio spread position. The breakeven points can be calculated using the following formulas:

Upper breakeven point = strike price of short calls
                        + (points of maximum profit/
                        number of uncovered calls)

Lower breakeven point = strike price of long call
                        ± net premium paid or received

Using the graph shown in Figure 5.11, since the maximum profit is $500, points of maximum profit are therefore equal to 5. Adding this to the higher strike of $45, we can calculate the breakeven point to be $50.

Conclusion

In this chapter, we covered a very nice spread of strategies that exploit volatility in an underlying asset. Remember to check the implied and historical volatility before investing in any option. I cannot stress this enough.

Remember that when the implied volatility is greater than the historical volatility, the option is going to be overvalued; this is optimal for selling options. On the other hand, when implied volatility is less than historical volatility, the option is going to be undervalued, and this is optimal for buying options.

In the next few chapters, I am going to cover the commodities, currency, and international markets. I'll explain the details of each and how investors can use these asset classes to diversify away from systematic risk and make some good money. But before I do that, let's go over a few arbitrage strategies that you can use to capture the occasional risk-free dollar.

Arbitrage Opportunities Using Options

In the options market, arbitrage trades are often performed by firm or floor traders to earn small profits with little or no risk. To set up an arbitrage, the options trader would go long on an underpriced position and sell the equivalent overpriced position.

If puts are overpriced relative to calls, the arbitrager would sell a naked put and offset it by buying a synthetic put. Similarly, when calls are overpriced in relation to puts, the arbitrager would sell a naked call and buy a synthetic call. The use of synthetic positions is common in options arbitrage strategies.

Arbitrage Strategies in Options Trading

The opportunity for arbitrage in options trading rarely exists for individual investors, as price discrepancies often appear only for a few moments. However, an important lesson to learn is that the actions by floor traders doing reversals and conversions quickly restore the market to equilibrium, keeping the price of calls and puts in line, establishing what is known as the put-call parity.

The Conversion

The Conversion Construction

Long 100 Shares
Buy 1 ATM Put
Sell 1 ATM Call

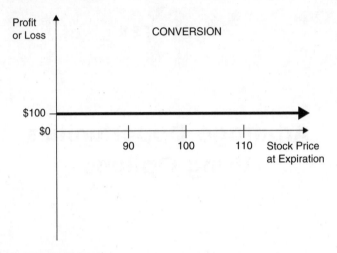

Figure 6.1   Conversion

A conversion is an arbitrage strategy in options trading that can be performed for a riskless profit when options are overpriced relative to the underlying stock. To do a conversion, the trader buys the underlying stock and offsets it with an equivalent synthetic short stock (long put + short call) position. (See Figure 6.1.)

Example   Suppose XYZ stock is trading at $100 in June, and the JUL 100 call is priced at $4, while the JUL 100 put is priced at $3. An arbitrage trader does a conversion by purchasing 100 shares of XYZ for $10,000 while simultaneously buying a JUL 100 put for $300 and selling a JUL 100 call for $400. The total cost to enter the trade is $10,000 + $300 − $400 = $9,900.

Assuming XYZ stock rallies to $110 in July, the long JUL 100 put will expire worthless, while the short JUL 100 call will expire in the money and will be assigned. The trader then sells his or her long stock for $10,000 as required. Since his or her cost is only $9,900, there is a $100 profit.

If instead, XYZ stock had dropped to $90 in July, the short JUL 100 call would expire worthless, while the long JUL 100 put would expire in the money. The trader would then exercise the long put to sell his or her long stock for $10,000, again netting a profit of $100.

Limited Risk-Free Profit Profit is locked in immediately when the conversion is done, and it can be computed using the following formula:

$$\text{Profit} = \text{strike price of call/put} - \text{purchase price of underlying}$$
$$+ \text{call premium} - \text{put premium}$$

Summary The conversion is used when options are overpriced. If the options are relatively underpriced, the reversal is used instead to perform the arbitrage trade.

The Reversal

The Reversal Composition
Short 100 Shares
Sell 1 ATM Put
Buy 1 ATM Call

A reversal, or reverse conversion, is an arbitrage strategy in options trading that can be performed for a riskless profit when options are underpriced relative to the underlying stock. To do a reversal, the trader short sells the underlying stock and offsets it with an equivalent synthetic long stock (long call + short put) position. (See Figure 6.2.)

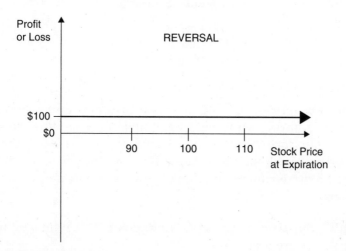

Figure 6.2 Reversal

Example   Suppose XYZ stock is trading at $100 in June, and the JUL 100 call is priced at $3, while the JUL 100 put is priced at $4. An arbitrage trader does a reversal by short selling 100 shares of XYZ for $10,000 while simultaneously buying a JUL 100 call for $300 and selling a JUL 100 put for $400. An initial credit of $10,100 is received when entering the trade.

If XYZ stock rallies to $110 in July, the short JUL 100 put will expire worthless, while the long JUL 100 call will expire in the money and will be exercised to cover the short stock position for $10,000. Since the initial credit received was $10,100, the trader ends up with a net profit of $100.

If instead, XYZ stock had dropped to $90 in July, the long JUL 100 call would expire worthless, while the short JUL 100 put would expire in the money and would be assigned. The trader would then buy back the obligated quantity of stock for $10,000 to cover his or her short stock position, again netting a profit of $100.

Limited Risk-Free Profit   Profit is locked in immediately when the reversal is done, and it can be calculated using the following formula:

$$\text{Profit} = \text{sale price of underlying} - \text{strike price of call/put}$$
$$+ \text{put premium} - \text{call premium}$$

Long Box

Long Box Composition
Buy 1 ITM Call
Sell 1 OTM Call
Buy 1 ITM Put
Sell 1 OTM Put

The box spread, or long box, is a common arbitrage strategy that involves buying a bull call spread together with the corresponding bear put spread, with both vertical spreads having the same strike prices and expiration dates. The long box is used when the spreads are underpriced in relation to their expiration values. (See Figure 6.3.)

Example   Suppose XYZ stock is trading at $45 in June, and the following prices are available:

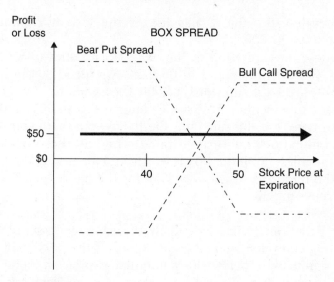

Figure 6.3   Long Box

JUL 40 put: $1.50

JUL 50 put: $6

JUL 40 call: $6

JUL 50 call: $1

Buying the bull call spread involves purchasing the JUL 40 call for $600 and selling the JUL 50 call for $100. The bull call spread costs: $600 − $100 = $500.

Buying the bear put spread involves purchasing the JUL 50 put for $600 and selling the JUL 40 put for $150. The bear put spread costs: $600 − $150 = $450.

The total cost of the box spread is: $500 + $450 = $950.

The expiration value of the box is computed to be: ($50 − $40) × 100 = $1,000.

Since the total cost of the box spread is less than its expiration value, a risk-free arbitrage is possible with the long box strategy. It can be observed that the expiration value of the box spread is indeed the difference between the strike prices of the options involved.

If XYZ stock remains unchanged at $45, then the JUL 40 put and the JUL 50 call expire worthless, while both the JUL 40 call and the JUL 50 put expire in the money, each with $500 in intrinsic value. So, the total value of the box at expiration is: $500 + $500 = $1,000.

Suppose on expiration in July, XYZ stock rallies to $50. Then, only the JUL 40 call expires in the money, with $1,000 in intrinsic value. So, the box is still worth $1,000 at expiration.

What happens when XYZ stock plummets to $40? A similar situation happens, but this time, it is the JUL 50 put that expires in the money with $1,000 in intrinsic value, while all the other options expire worthless. Still, the box is worth $1,000.

As the trader had paid only $950 for the entire box, his or her profit comes to $50.

Limited Risk-Free Profit   Essentially, the arbitrager is simply buying and selling equivalent spreads, and as long as the price paid for the box is significantly below the combined expiration value of the spreads, a riskless profit can be locked in immediately. It can be calculated using the following formulas:

Expiration value of box = higher-strike price − lower-strike price

Risk-free profit = expiration value of box − net premium paid

Summary   The box spread is profitable when the component spreads are underpriced. Conversely, when the box is overpriced, you can sell the box for a profit. This strategy is known as a short box.

Short Box

Short Box Composition
Sell 1 ITM Call
Buy 1 OTM Call
Sell 1 ITM Put
Buy 1 OTM Put

The short box is an arbitrage strategy that involves selling a bull call spread together with the corresponding bear put spread with the same strike prices and expiration dates. The short box is a strategy that is used when the spreads are overpriced with respect to their combined expiration value. (See Figure 6.4.)

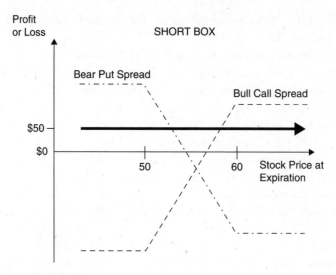

Figure 6.4   Short Box

Example   Suppose XYZ stock is trading at $55 in July, and the following prices are available:

AUG 50 put: $2

AUG 60 put: $7

AUG 50 call: $7

AUG 60 call: $1.50

Selling the bull call spread involves shorting the AUG 50 call for $700 while buying the AUG 60 call for $150. The premium collected from the sale of the bull call spread is: $700 − $150 = $550.

Selling the bear put spread involves shorting the AUG 60 put for $700 while buying the AUG 50 put for $200. The premium collected from the sale of the bear put spread comes to: $700 − $200 = $500.

Together, the net premium received for shorting the box is: $550 + $500 = $1,050.

Since the total price of the box spread is more than its expiration value, a risk-free arbitrage is possible using the short box strategy. Selling the box will result in a net premium received of $1,050. It can be observed that the expiration value of the box spread is indeed the difference between the strike prices of the options involved. The expiration value of the box is computed to be: ($50 − $40) × 100 = $1,000.

If XYZ stock remains unchanged at $55, then the AUG 50 put and the AUG 60 call expire worthless, while both the AUG 50 call and the AUG 60 put expire in the money, each with $500 in intrinsic value. So, the total value of the box at expiration is: $500 + $500 = $1,000.

Suppose on expiration in August, XYZ stock rallies to $60. Then, only the AUG 50 call expires in the money, with $1,000 in intrinsic value. So, the box is still worth $1,000 at expiration.

So, what happens when XYZ stock plunges to $50? A similar situation occurs, but this time, it is the AUG 60 put that expires in the money with $1,000 in intrinsic value, while all the other options expire worthless. Hence, the box is still worth $1,000.

As the trader had collected $1,050 for shorting the box, his or her profit comes to $50 after buying it back for $1,000 on expiration date.

Limited Risk-Free Profit   Basically, with the short box, the arbitrager is just buying and selling equivalent spreads, and as long as the net premium obtained for selling the two spreads is significantly higher than the combined expiration value of the spreads, a risk-free profit can be captured upon entering the trade. It can be calculated using the following formulas:

Expiration value of box = higher-strike price − lower-strike price

Risk-free profit = net premium received − expiration value of box

Dividend Arbitrage

Dividend arbitrage is an arbitrage strategy whereby the options trader buys both the stock and the equivalent number of put options before ex-dividend and waits to collect the dividend before exercising his or her put.

Example   Suppose XYZ stock is trading at $90 and is paying $2 in dividend tomorrow. A put with a striking price of $100 is selling for $11. The options trader can enter a riskless dividend arbitrage by purchasing both the stock for $9,000 and the put for $1,100 for a total of $10,100.

On ex-dividend, he or she collects $200 in the form of dividends and exercises his or her put to sell his or her stock for $10,000, bringing in a total of $10,200. Since his or her initial investment is only $10,100, he or she earns $100 in zero-risk profits.

Dividend Capturing Using Covered Calls

Some stocks pay generous dividends every quarter. You qualify for the dividend if you are holding on the shares before the ex-dividend date.

Many people have tried to buy the shares just before the ex-dividend date simply to collect the dividend payout, only to find that the stock price drops by at least the amount of the dividend after the ex-dividend date, effectively nullifying the earnings from the dividend itself.

There is, however, a way to go about collecting the dividends using options. On the day before ex-dividend date, you can do a covered write by buying the dividend-paying stock while simultaneously writing an equivalent number of deep-in-the-money call options on it. The call strike price plus the premiums received should be equal to or greater than the current stock price.

On ex-dividend date, assuming no assignment takes place, you will have qualified for the dividend. While the underlying stock price will have dropped by the dividend amount, the written call options will also register the same drop, since deep-in-the-money options have a delta of nearly 1. You can then sell the underlying stock, buy back the short calls at no loss, and wait to collect the dividends.

The risk in using this strategy is that of an early assignment taking place before the ex-dividend date. If assigned, you will not be able to qualify for the dividends. Hence, you should ensure that the premiums received when selling the call options take into account all transaction costs that will be involved, in case such an assignment does occur.

Example   In November, XYZ Company has declared that it is paying cash dividends of $1.50 on December 1. One day before the ex-dividend date, XYZ stock is trading at $50, while a DEC 40 call option is priced at $10.20. An options trader decides to play for dividends by purchasing 100 shares of XYZ stock for $5,000 and simultaneously writing a DEC 40 covered call for $1,020.

On ex-dividend date, the stock price of XYZ drops by $1.50 to $48.50. Similarly, the price of the written DEC 40 call option also drops by the same amount to $8.70.

As he or she had already qualified for the dividend payout, the options trader decides to exit the position by selling the long stock and buying back the call options. Selling the stock for $4,850 results in a $150 loss on the long stock position, while buying back the call for $870 results in a gain of $150 on the short option position.

As you can see, the profit and loss of both positions cancel out each other. All the profit attainable from this strategy comes from the dividend payout, which is $150.

Conclusion

As I said before, arbitrage opportunities are difficult to find and are usually exploited by advanced computer programs at investment banks. But if you ever happen upon one, by all means, apply one of the preceding techniques and make some free money.

Now that I have covered all the ways to maximize profits using options in bull markets, bear markets, high- and low-volatility situations, and arbitrage positions, I am going to go over some different types of markets that you can apply these strategies to.

Next to the equities market, the commodities and currency markets tend to be a very active options arenas—which brings me to my next chapter: the FOREX market.

CHAPTER 7

The FOREX Market: Secrets of a Currency Trader

We have all seen those FOREX commercials on TV—touting currency as the new wild west of investments. A market where anyone can make a buck. A market that doesn't close at 4 PM, but pushes through the night for the strong willed.

Well, before you buy into the hype and sink $50,000 in Euro—read this chapter and gain an understanding of gears work. The FOREX market is a complicated beast with a lot of in's, out's, and what have you's … You don't want to be caught with your pants down when hunting profits in this environment.

FOREX Basics: What FOREX Is All About

In the foreign exchange (FOREX) market, there are no companies to own for the purposes of capital gains or dividend payouts. Neither are there bonds nor debentures to trade in return for interest payments and the eventual return of your cash.

Instead, it's all about exchanging one kind of currency for another. In fact, if there was only one currency in the world, there would be no FOREX market.

If you've traveled abroad, the chances are good that you've been a FOREX market participant yourself. The last time you went on a vacation to a foreign country, you probably exchanged some of your own currency for the local variety. The FOREX counter at the local airport, hotel, or bank took your U.S. dollars (or whatever you brought with you) and gave you X amount of the local currency.

If you had some of the local currency remaining at the end of your vacation, you changed it back into your own currency before going home.

Here's the important thing: If you were paying attention to both transactions, you probably noticed that the rate of exchange between your U.S. dollars and the local currency was slightly different each way.

That difference in rates is the entire basis for the FOREX market's existence and the reason why you as a speculator can make good profits if you know what you're doing.

Why the FOREX Market Exists

Before we go into money-making opportunities, let's take a closer look at why the FOREX market exists on a global basis. It's much bigger than your currency exchange experience while on vacation, but it's the same general principle in action.

The global FOREX market is all about greasing the wheels of global business. A large international company buying in one country and selling in another must make a corresponding purchase and sale in each country's respective currency, too.

The identity of those banks doing the trading isn't really important to you as a private speculator, though. Unless you're a big institution with a lot of large FOREX transactions to make, you'll never be talking to the trading desk at any of these big players.

However, it is important to know that there's no central exchange for any of these banks to agree on prices. There's no FOREX equivalent of the New York Stock Exchange (NYSE).

Instead, one bank quotes a bid/ask for a given currency, another bank decides to quote what it feels is a more competitive bid/ask, yet another tries to beat the other two, and so on.

The end result is that there may be several bid and ask prices around the globe for the very same currency pair at any one time. But in the age of the rapid data exchange via the Internet and other networks, those interbank price differences are smaller than ever and change with lightning speed.

They do this in the interbank market, which is composed of large international banks. Global heavyweights such as Deutsche Bank,

UBS AG, Barclays Capital, Citi, Royal Bank of Scotland, J.P. Morgan Chase, HSBC, and several others make up the bulk of the currency market.[1]

The banks aren't doing all this out of charity, of course. They make their money between their individual bid and ask spreads as market makers. Buy low and sell high is their mantra, and the difference represents their profit margin. Without it, there would be no incentive for banks to make a market in the world's currencies.

However, electronic data transfer—especially the Internet—has revolutionized the FOREX market by ensuring that those bid/ask spreads are more competitive than ever before.

It's also ensured that the FOREX market has grown by leaps and bounds and has provided retail speculators the chance to participate in an exciting new speculative opportunity.

How Large and Liquid Is the FOREX Market?

The bond market dwarfs the stock market in terms of sheer size. But the FOREX market is the king of all when it comes to volume, liquidity, and geographical dispersion. Participants include central banks, major global banks, currency speculators, corporations, governments, and other financial institutions.

According to recent figures from the Bank for International Settlements (BIS; published in its Triennial Central Bank Survey in December 2007), the average daily turnover in global FOREX markets is a staggering $3.2 trillion.[2] By comparison, daily turnover at the NYSE was a mere $119 billion as of December 2007.[3]

London accounts for 34.1 percent of all FOREX trade, with New York (16.6 percent) and Tokyo (6 percent) the other FOREX powerhouses, according to the BIS.[4]

As the biggest fish in the sea, the top-tier interbank market accounts for 53 percentof the volume overall.[5] Next in the pecking order are smaller investment banks, multinational corporations, hedge funds, and retail-level market makers. (These market makers are the ones you'll be dealing with as an individual retail FOREX trader.)

Retail traders are beginning to make their presence felt and now comprise more than 2 percent of the global market by volume.[6] That may not seem like a lot, but it works out to approximately

$50 to $60 billion a day—that's *one-third or more* of the NYSE dollar volume.

What's more, a 2007 report from Aite Group claims that retail FOREX trader volume should now be over $100 billion a day.[6] The NYSE's daily trading volume will be exceeded in the next two or three years at present growth rates.

And that's for a retail market that was all but nonexistent even two decades ago: Retail FOREX trading began in 1996 with primitive trading platforms offered by a variety of dealers. (These weren't very efficient, and it was the early 2000s before recognizable trading platforms such as *Metaquotes* came into existence.)

In fact, only in the last two or three years have truly modern FOREX trading platforms developed to the point where they're as user friendly as more well-known stock trading software.

What's behind this staggering growth rate for retail FOREX traders?

- Very low transaction costs: Commissions are low or nonexistent, meaning you can pay only the spread to trade a given currency pair.
- Unparalleled liquidity: There is never a shortage of liquidity in the world's largest trading market.
- Generous trading hours: The FOREX market trades 24 hours a day, from 22:00 UTC on Sunday until 22:00 UTC on Friday. (UTC stands for Universal Time, Coordinated and is roughly equivalent to Greenwich Mean Time [GMT].)
- Exceptional leverage: It's not uncommon to trade the FOREX market using 100:1 leverage.

To summarize, FOREX trading for the retail investor is one of the fastest growing sectors out there.

I'll discuss each of the possible ways to get involved in FOREX in just a moment, but first, it's important to understand some of the specialized terminology involved.

Understanding Currency Pairs, Pips, and Other Basic FOREX Terminology

To measure the value of something, you need to compare it to something else.

This is easy for non-FOREX investments, as you simply measure the worth of your stock, option, bond, future, and so forth in terms of your own currency. There's no mystery about valuing a stock price that's moved by $1, for example.

But in FOREX, there's not really such a thing as "your own currency." Instead, there's a *base currency* against which another *quoted currency* is linked to form a *currency pair*.

- In the EURUSD currency pair, the USD is the base currency, and the EUR is the quoted currency valued against it in terms of U.S. dollars.
- In the USDJPY currency pair, the JPY is the base currency, and the USD is the quoted currency valued against it in terms of Japanese yen.

Table 7.1 shows the most popular currency pairs in the FOREX market.

The trading volume of each currency pair shown in Table 7.1 is roughly in proportion to its position on the table. The EURUSD

Table 7.1　Popular Currency Pairs in the FOREX Market

Symbol	Currency Pair	Trading Terminology
EURUSD	Euro/U.S. Dollar	"Euro"
USDJPY	U.S. Dollar/Japanese Yen	"Dollar Yen"
GBPUSD	British Pound/U.S. Dollar	"Cable"
USDCHF	U.S. Dollar/Swiss Franc	"Dollar Swiss" or "Swissie"
USDCAD	U.S. Dollar/Canadian Dollar	"Dollar Canada"
AUDUSD	Australian Dollar/U.S. Dollar	"Aussie Dollar"
EURGBP	Euro/British Pound	"Euro Sterling"
EURJPY	Euro/Japanese Yen	"Euro Yen"
EURCHF	Euro/Swiss Franc	"Euro Swiss"
GBPCHF	British Pound/Swiss Franc	"Sterling Swiss"
GBPJPY	British Pound/Japanese Yen	"Sterling Yen"
CHFJPY	Swiss Franc/Japanese Yen	"Swiss Yen"
NZDUZD	New Zealand Dollar/U.S. Dollar	"New Zealand Dollar" or "Kiwi"
USDZAR	U.S. Dollar/South African Rand	"Dollar Zar" or "South African Rand"
GLDUSD	Spot Gold	"Gold"
SLVUSD	Spot Silver	"Silver"

contract is the most liquid and a good place to start studying the FOREX market once you're ready.

A currency pair that doesn't involve your own currency is known as a *cross-rate*. If you deal in U.S. dollars, the EURGBP currency pair would be considered a cross-rate, as no U.S. dollars are traded in the transaction. However, EURGBP would *not* be considered a cross-rate from the perspective of someone regularly dealing in euros or British pounds.

There's another word used in FOREX that you may not have seen before: a *pip*. A pip is usually the smallest increment of price change in a currency pair.

- For the EURUSD pair, a one-pip change would be a movement from 1.4000 to 1.4001.
- A corresponding one-pip change in USDJPY would be from 99.50 to 99.51.

Notes

In some electronic-dealing networks, you'll sometimes observe prices changing in tenths of pips.

But normally, this level of fine-tuned price competition doesn't occur in retail-level trading quotes.

The concept of pips is important to understand, because FOREX bid/ask spreads are typically quoted in terms of pips. Most retail dealers offer a two or three pip spread on the EURUSD, by way of example.

Another FOREX-specific term is the *big figure*. The numbers farther to the left in a price quote are typically known as big figures (e.g., 1.4099 changing to 1.4100, or 2.0000 changing to 1.9999). These big figures often act as resistance or support levels during trading.

There are a couple more useful FOREX trading terms to know, but it will be simpler to discuss them when covering the essentials of FOREX contracts and FOREX trading in the next section.

Spot FOREX Margin Power: Trading $100,000 with Only a $1,000 Deposit

If you're a skillful trader or seeking to become one, FOREX trading offers what's probably the fastest way to make a lot of money due to its exceptional leverage opportunities.

Conversely, you can *lose* a lot of money very quickly if you don't know what you're doing.

That's all due to leverage, which is best explained as the concept of having a *small* amount of money do *a lot* of work for you. Depending on which online broker you choose to open your account with, you can trade with up to 500:1 leverage in FOREX. This is fairly extreme, however, and most firms will allow "only" 100:1 leverage.

That 100:1 leverage should be plenty, though. It means that for every $100,000 face value of the contracts you wish to control, you need only commit $1,000 from your trading account; this is referred to as a margin account.

Margin is essentially a good faith deposit showing that you can honor your trading obligations without imposing risk on your counterparty (normally a market maker or a clearing firm). It's the minimum account balance you must hold to continue controlling a given amount of contracts. If your account balance falls below that magic number ($1,000 in the case of a $100,000 contract), you'll be immediately subject to a margin call, which is a notification that more funds are needed to cover your position(s).

Naturally, in real-life trading, you would want to be holding substantially more than the minimum 100:1 margin in your account. Otherwise, the very first price movement against you would result in a margin call.

A good rule of thumb is to have at least three times the minimum margin in your account, preferably four. This means that your *effective* leverage is 33:1 or 25:1 rather than the official 100:1 leverage when trading FOREX. Anything less than that is playing with fire, and you want to be a successful trader, not a failure.

Risk management is extremely important in all kinds of trading, but it's especially critical in FOREX, where the leverage is so high and the price can change direction 24 hours a day, from 22:00 UTC on Sunday until 22:00 UTC on Friday.

We'll delve more closely into FOREX risk management later in this chapter, but for now, be aware that the 100:1 leverage ratio represents the level where you would normally be expecting margin calls and not the level at which you'll realistically be making (or losing) money.

The Differences between Trading FOREX and Other Markets

The main differences between trading FOREX and any other markets can best be summarized by the following list:

1. The very high leverage offered to retail traders (frequently 100:1, as previously discussed)
2. A true 24-hour global market that never closes between 22:00 UTC on Sunday and 22:00 UTC on Friday (discussed in the preceding section in this chapter)
3. Daily rollover of spot contracts
4. No centralized regulation of spot FOREX brokers and dealers
5. Global trading platforms, where you might be using the exact same software as someone in Brazil, Russia, China, or Australia

We'll cover each of the last three points in this section, but first, let's talk about FOREX spot contracts and how they're a bit different from what you might have seen before.

How Spot FOREX Contracts Work

The definition of a spot foreign exchange contract reads something like this: "a binding obligation to buy or sell a specific sum of foreign currency at the current market rate, for settlement in two business days' time."

In other words, spot contracts are for short-term trading only. If you hold a spot contract for three business days, you'll be settling it, which is to say that you would be expected to actually fulfill the transaction of (for example) exchanging $100,000 U.S. dollars for *X* amount of the other currency.

This would not be a good situation. After all, it's unlikely that you would actually *have* $100,000 available for this settlement if your trading account is only the $3,000 to $4,000 or so that I recommend for trading a $100,000 face-value contract. Not only would *you* be feeling some pain, but the party on the other side would not particularly like being subjected to that risk of default.

So, to avoid this potentially unpleasant situation, the concept of a *daily rollover* is implemented at the close of each trading day. New York–based firms typically use midnight Eastern Standard Time (EST) as their trading-day close, and your account will be temporarily inaccessible for about five minutes after this point. (End-of-day times will vary for companies located elsewhere on the globe.)

At the end of each trading day, your existing FOREX spot position is rolled over into a new position. Your existing contracts are sold and replacement contracts bought. You are now in *new* contracts with the day's profits and losses locked in. You need not worry about settlement should you hold the position for several days or even weeks.

The price at which you "sold" and at which you "bought" is not always identical, however.

While you don't pay a commission or a spread for rollover, there is an interest rate debit (or credit) applied. This is due to the different interest rates that prevail for different currencies.

Let's illustrate this with a simple example:

Contract: $100,000 EURUSD spot

Spot rate: 1.4123 EUR for each USD

USD interest rate: 3 percent

EUR interest rate: 2.5 percent

If you bought the base currency USD (thereby selling the quoted currency EUR), you would get paid for holding USD:

$$(100,000 \times 1.41 \times 3\% \times 1/360) = \$11.75$$

This is a *credit* to you for holding U.S. dollars. However, you have also sold euros to do this (remember, you're exchanging one currency for another in FOREX), so you have a *debit*, too:

$$(100,000 \times 1.41 \times 2.5\% \times 1/360) = \$9.79$$

Your *net credit* in this case would be: $11.75 − $9.79 = $1.96.

If you had taken the opposite position on this contract, you would pay a *net debit* of $1.96 for rolling over a long EUR/short USD position.

Please note that this number is *irrespective of any profit or loss you've taken on the actual price movement of the pair* while you've been holding it until rollover. The rollover is simply a debit (or credit) for holding the pair to the close of the trading day.

If your broker or dealer follows the preceding rollover interest rate method, the price of your new spot contract will be identical to the old one. If the price at rollover was 1.4123, that's the price at which you bought or sold the new one.

Some firms don't bother with cash-based credits and debits for daily rollovers. Instead, they charge (or credit) you pips or fractions thereof for rollovers. Instead of a cash difference in your account, your new contract would be bought (or sold) at a pip difference.

Perhaps your existing contract was sold at 1.4123 and the new one bought at 1.4124 if there was an interest rate debit for that pair (you "lost" a pip on your new long position to cover that debit). If you were due a credit instead, you might get 1.4122 and therefore "gain" a pip on your long position in this example.

The actual pip difference and debit/credit property is determined by the interest rates and whether you were long or short that particular contract.

The good news is that now that you understand how rollover calculations work, you don't need to worry about them. Your broker/dealer does them automatically, and your only inconvenience will be not being able to enter/cancel orders during the rollover period, which is several minutes after the close of day.

If you're a day trader and never hold a position during your firm's close-of-day time, you'll never see a rollover take place in your account.

Who Regulates the Global Spot FOREX Markets?

In a word: nobody.

Notes

Meanwhile, in the United Kingdom and Australia, the Financial Services Authority (FSA) and Australian Securities and Investment Commission (ASIC) oversee the same FOREX regulatory areas in their respective jurisdictions.

European Union countries and Switzerland have similar institutions of their own.

The global, decentralized nature of spot FOREX means that the market as a whole is essentially a free-for-all in terms of broker/dealer practices, conduct, and ethics.

While the National Futures Association (NFA) and the Commodity Futures Trading Commission (CFTC) have some say over U.S. FOREX dealers, their powers are not extraordinary and limit only the worst problems such as insufficiently capitalized companies and outright theft of client funds.

The CFTC has the authority to close any unregulated entity in the retail FOREX industry, whereas the NFA enforces certain capital requirements and sound financial structures.

However, the level of regulation is such that you don't have quite the same level of consumer protection that exists in more established markets.

You therefore need to be quite careful about investigating the reputation of any spot FOREX firm you're considering for an account.

Complaints about less-than-ethical spot FOREX broker/dealer practices include the following:

- Large amounts of slippage (exceptionally bad fills on trade orders)
- Running stops (pushing the price up and down to clear out customer stops before returning the market to "normal")
- Faulty communications (the firm's online network becoming suspiciously unreliable when trying to change orders or close out trades)
- Bid/ask spreads that widen to exceptional levels during and after crucial news releases (usually running out stops in the process or otherwise making the market very difficult to trade)

There are, in fact, some very well-run spot FOREX broker/dealers out there, of course.

But do conduct *thorough* research on the Internet (including the web sites of the regulatory authorities themselves) before committing any funds to a given spot FOREX organization.

Spot FOREX Trading Platforms

As a retail trader, you have two main options when it comes to a trading platform that will chart and/or facilitate trading on the spot FOREX market.

Proprietary Software A number of spot FOREX brokers and dealers offer their own proprietary platform. As you might expect, this can be both good and bad. Some firms may have exceptionally good programmers to create good software; others don't.

Key points to consider are the flexibility and breadth of charting functions; the ease with which you can enter, change, and cancel orders; and how easy it is to configure the visual layout to meet your personal preferences.

The only way to test any such software is to download it and try a demo account. If the software feels awkward, offers limited functionality in areas you feel are important, and/or you get consistently bad fills even in demo mode, you're better off looking for a more suitable alternative.

It may seem too obvious, but one thing you must master on unfamiliar user interfaces is how to enter your intended order correctly.

It can be all too easy to enter a stop order in place of a limit order (or go long rather than short) if you're not *very* careful about where you click your mouse on a proprietary trading platform. Mistakes can and do happen, especially if the software allows "one-click trading." Make those mistakes on a demo account in the initial learning curve.

MetaTrader 4 (Soon to Be MetaTrader 5) This program is pretty much the de facto standard for FOREX trading. Available as a free download from the MetaTrader web site and numerous different spot FOREX brokers and dealers, you can't help but cross paths with this program during *any* online FOREX research.

The MetaTrader layout is not quite as configurable and customizable as it could be (for example, the zoom levels leave a lot to be desired), but otherwise, it's an extremely flexible option with unparalleled user support.

In fact, the very large user community is a major plus, as MetaTrader's MQL4 programming language makes it possible for you to create and customize your own scripts, alerts, indicators, and also Expert Advisors (automated trading programs).

Even if you don't feel like programming your own algorithms, a huge library of basic and sophisticated code is available for free or for a fee at MetaTrader user forums and MQL4 programming outfits.

So, although the product is "standard" across the industry, it's quite feasible to tinker with a vast library of add-ons to create a truly unique trading system or method for spot FOREX.

For your first demo-trading experience, selecting MetaTrader 4 would be a good choice. You can always try one of the proprietary platforms later to see where it might be stronger or weaker than MetaTrader itself.

As of this writing, MetaTrader 5 (and the corresponding MQL5 programming language) has not yet been in open release.

However, it might well be the new standard by the time you read this book.

The Difference between Brokers and Dealing Desks

Prior to starting live FOREX trading, you need to decide whether to go with a broker or a dealer. Table 7.2 compares one against the other.

At first glance, it may seem a great thing not to be paying commissions on every FOREX trade you make. But on closer inspection, it's not necessarily a great deal, because dealers have to earn their money somehow. You pay for their services in a different form.

You'll find that dealer bid/ask spreads will be significantly wider than brokers—often by at least one pip, perhaps two. Over many trades, that difference can add up to much more than the commissions charged by brokers.

Fixed spreads from dealers will be constant unless there's news (often in the form of a central bank announcement or a major economic report) that moves the markets very rapidly. In those instances,

Table 7.2 Brokers versus Dealers

Key Point	Brokers	Dealers
Commissions Charged	Yes	No
Maintain Fixed Bid/Ask Spreads	No	Yes, with the spread often widening during news
Operate a Dealing Desk	Not usually	Yes
Manage an Electronic Communications Network (ECN)	Often, if not always	No
Act as the Counterparty or Principal to Customer Transactions	Not usually	Often, if not always
Use MetaTrader 4 Software	Not usually	Often

the spreads will widen significantly in all affected pairs. This can have disastrous consequences for your trading, as the spread may widen to exceed your stop, and suddenly, you're out of the market.

Generally speaking, it's a bad idea to be in the market when it's rocketing or plummeting in response to news (more on this in a later section of this chapter on trading), not least because dealers have been known to exploit this phenomenon quite ruthlessly.

Another disadvantage of dealers is that many of them operate a dealing desk as a market maker, which means that they may frequently be taking the other side of your trades. Would you care to guess what happens to your trades if you begin winning (and thereby taking money from the dealer)? Your trades get filled at bad prices, your stops get run (with the evidence magically erased from your charts after the deed is done), your orders sometimes go unexecuted, and so forth.

This is the dark and ugly side of spot FOREX trading and a consequence of the rather lax regulation of FOREX dealers.

However, not *all* dealers are this unethical, and some will operate fairly by making their money honestly from their fixed bid/ask spreads. You'll need to carefully research which dealers have a good reputation on FOREX trading boards/forums and make your decisions accordingly.

In my opinion, though, you're ultimately better off with a firm that does *not* operate a dealing desk and that instead offers an electronic communications network.

Why You Should Consider Trading via ECN Brokers

An electronic communications network is about the best deal you can get as a retail trader. An ECN is essentially a marketplace where multiple market makers, banks, and traders enter competing bids and offers into a centralized platform.

There is no fixed spread, and *everyone* functions as a market maker of sorts. The best bid and offer on the ECN is always on display and constantly evolves. (In fact, you can narrow the spread *yourself* by making a bid higher than the existing bid or an offer lower than the existing ask. Of course, your moment of glory normally lasts only a moment or two, until your order is filled or someone moves the bid/ask away from you.)

In an ECN, all trades are done in the name of the ECN broker, and you are completely anonymous, thus avoiding the problem of trading against a single counterparty that has a vested interest in you not winning their money from them. Your counterparties in an ECN are various liquidity providers or other traders, not one centralized dealer.

Brokers that do not offer an ECN but instead promote themselves as no dealing desk (NDD) brokers offer many of the same features, but the market making is not quite as transparent as with an ECN.

Demo versus Live Accounts

The last thing you need to know about the mechanics of actually getting into spot FOREX trading concerns account types.

A demo account is one where an amount of fictitious money is supplied to an account and you trade on the broker/dealer's demo network until the account expires. (Normally, this is 30 days.) In almost all cases, this demo network will be identical to the live network, except that (1) your orders don't actually get filled by live counterparties (obviously), and (2) the demo network may experience a few glitches that the live network doesn't, as the demo network is not as well maintained. Some firms even do some of their software testing on the demo network, making it occasionally unreliable or dysfunctional.

This means that a demo network may not always provide a truly accurate measurement of how stable the platform is or how the broker or dealer executes live orders.

The main purpose of a demo account is to get you accustomed to using the trading platform and then to establish some kind of profitable trading method. However, many people have claimed that trading with fake money is not good enough practice for trading with your own hard-earned cash and that you should move to a live account as early as possible to truly begin learning to trade.

Standard, Mini-, and Microaccounts

There are three levels of live accounts: standard, mini-, and microaccounts.

Standard accounts offer trading at the standard lot (contract) level. A standard contract normally has a face value of USD $100,000 or its equivalent in another currency.

Miniaccounts offer mini-lot trading ($10,000 lots), and micro-accounts deal primarily with $1,000 lots. With a microaccount, you can get started with an account minimum of $500 (sometimes even less) and get a feel for spot FOREX trading without excessive risk. Your 100:1 margin goes a long way, so keep in mind good money management rules, even at the microlevel.

Generally speaking, if you can make money *consistently* at the microlevel, you can do the same at the mini- and standard level.

And unless you have a lot of money to risk, starting to trade at the microlevel will keep your losses relatively small until you get the hang of trading FOREX. It's better to do most of your losing at the microlevel, where the pain is less.

After all, you can always add more money to your account and upgrade it when you feel more confident about risking larger sums of capital.

Trading Strategies in FOREX: Trading Effectively to Make Money from Currency Fluctuations

When trading FOREX, a good rule of thumb is to risk no more than 2 to 3 percent of your account in any one trade, *including* commissions and possible slippage. Keeping to that level will ensure that you won't wipe out your account, even if you suffer a bad string of losses, and yet you'll still grow your account nicely with an "edge" that ensures you continue to win over the long run.

How do you develop an edge? You develop an edge by devising a trading method that generates more profits than losses after all expenses have been considered. Deciding when to enter and exit the market is absolutely crucial to your success.

But before you can develop a method, you need to objectively study the market. And just like any other asset class, FOREX trading analysis can be divided into two schools:

1. Fundamental analysis (valuing what a given currency should be worth, given a set of economic circumstances and outlooks)
2. Technical analysis (reading a chart of past price performance to determine future performance)

You may have heard the old adage that in the short term, the market behaves like a voting machine, and in the long term, it acts like a weighing machine.

Fundamental analysis is the weighing machine, while technical analysis is its voting equivalent. Both can make you money, but the time frames are often completely different.

If you're trading *spot FOREX* contracts, you'll most likely be a short-term trader, and therefore technical analysis will act as your main guide.

If you're trading *currency futures or options,* you'll probably be looking at a longer time frame, and fundamental analysis will play a greater role in your trading. It's not easy to evaluate an entire country as to how its economy (and therefore currency) will fare, but if you devote enough time, you can develop quite a comprehensive picture of where the numbers should go over the long term.

A full discussion of such detailed fundamental analysis is beyond the scope of this chapter, but suffice it to say that you'll be doing a lot of reading and number crunching to form strong enough conclusions that would merit a long-term trade based on fundamentals.

Short-term traders have it a bit easier, at least in terms of reading reports and journals.

However, even day traders need to pay attention to at least *some* FOREX market fundamentals.

At the very least, you must be aware of when the day's major economic reports are being released. The dates and times of these releases are critical, as the price of a given currency may move spectacularly if the numbers aren't what the market expected.

Some people actually "trade the news" by trying to hop on and then off the profit train as the market erupts in one direction or another. This might work for you, but it requires rapid reflexes and nerves of steel, plus a dealer that can fill your orders during such fast-moving market conditions. (Be warned that some dealers refuse to accept accounts where the trading method revolves around very rapid news-oriented trades.)

There are numerous Internet sites that will have a current listing of upcoming U.S. economic events including the release times of such reports as the Non-Farm Payrolls, the Purchasing Managers' Index (PMI), the Consumer Price Index (CPI), retail sales, and durable goods. Some sites have report listings for *all* major countries with a strong FOREX market presence, and you can pick and choose which items are of most interest to your chosen currency pair(s).

Find an economic calendar site you like, bookmark it, and refer to it frequently. Otherwise, you'll be victimized by a brutal price movement that came out of the blue because you had no idea a crucial report was being released just then.

Two excellent sites include: www.forexeconomiccalendar.com and www.forexfactory.com/calendar.php—this site allows you to customize to your time zone.

Some days and weeks are busier than others, but never assume that a day will be quiet just because nothing happened the last time a particular report was released.

The Most Effective Technical Indicators for Trading FOREX

In the absence of sudden market-moving news, the price of a given currency pair exists in one of two states: It's either trending or locked in a range. Determining when it's about to move from one state to the other is in fact the holy grail of successful technical trading, because there are indicators that work extremely well for one phase but not another.

For example, trending indicators such as moving averages and Moving Average Convergence Divergence (MACD) work well for keeping you in trends, but they're useless when no trend exists due to the excessive false signals they generate.

The reverse is true for oscillators such as Stochastics, which accurately call tops and bottoms during range-bound intervals only.

Still others such as Fibonacci retracements/extensions and pivot points are useful for identifying likely support and resistance but can sometimes be ambiguous about their signals.

Here's one thing you must keep in mind besides news releases: FOREX tends to move sharply off support and resistance more frequently than stocks, so that must be considered when developing an appropriate trading system. Also, be warned that very powerful trends can develop and sustain themselves, despite your best efforts to accurately fade the market.

When devising a consistently successful system, you can minimize the weaknesses of various kinds of indicators by incorporating several different types at once.

First, let's look at each kind of indicator in turn.

All charts show the EURUSD pair tracked by 15-minute candlesticks. (These are only brief examples to show you actual FOREX price charts and how certain indicators work to predict prices.)

Simple and Exponential Moving Averages

A moving average is nothing more than a trend-following indicator. Simple moving averages are (as the name suggests) simple arithmetical averages taken of the most recent closing prices, whereas exponential moving averages are weighted so that the most recent data is exponentially more important.

Many people use more than one at a time to generate crossovers between the averages. There are times when these provide useful entry or exit points.

As you can see from Figure 7.1, moving-average crossovers work well when the market is trending ($A - B$ and $C - D$), but they're ineffective when there is no real trend ($B - C$).

Also, note that exponential moving averages tend to hug the price closely. This means that compared to simple moving averages, (1) the price is less likely to swing very far from the moving average, and (2) the price tends to break above or below the moving average less frequently.

This may be helpful or a hindrance, depending on how you're attempting to trade.

In general, you want to be short when the price is below the average and long when it's above average. A good entry point for placing FOREX trades is when there's a pullback right to the average. That way, you can place your stop not far on the other side if the trend fails and crashes back through.

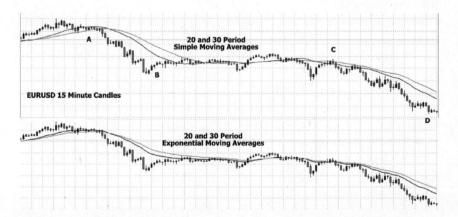

Figure 7.1   Comparison of Simple and Exponential Moving Averages in a Simple Crossover Setup

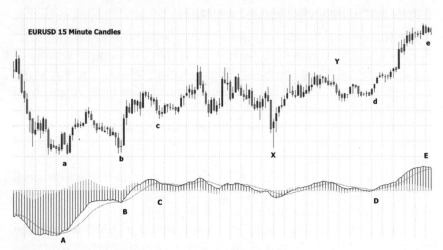

EURUSD 15 Minute Candles

Figure 7.2   Using MACD to Predict FOREX Prices

However, this is a lot less likely to work when the moving averages are flat and there's no slope to their lines. Save this kind of trading for when a trend has already shown its hand.

Moving Average Convergence Divergence

As you might expect from an indicator based on moving averages, MACD is a trend-following indicator and is shown in Figure 7.2. You can use crossovers between the two moving averages to get you into trends $(D - E)$ at the expense of many false signals $(C - D)$ when there is no trend.

Moving Average Convergence Divergence is slightly more sophisticated than a simple crossover indicator, however.

Examine the interval $A - B$ on the chart. You'll see that MACD is rising, while the price $(a - b)$ interval is flat on the actual price chart. There's even a double bottom on the price.

When you see this kind of divergence between MACD and the price, it's a good sign that the price is going to rise and follow MACD. (The inverse is true if MACD is falling and the price is level.)

The more notable the divergence is, the stronger the signal will be. This kind of divergence is also notable with the Stochastic oscillator, which we'll also examine.

One more note: Buying at X and selling at Y was a good trade in the middle of the static trading range $C - D$. Moving Average

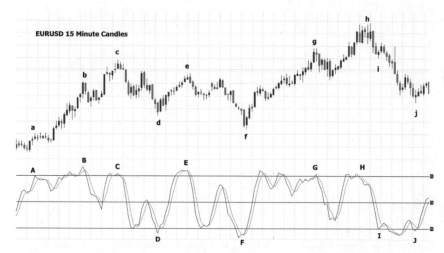

Figure 7.3   Using the Stochastic Oscillator to Predict FOREX Prices

Convergence Divergence can still help you if there's a strong reversal candle (as with point *X*) followed by a crossover.

Stochastic Oscillator

As mentioned earlier, the Stochastic indicator works well only during choppy markets where there is no clear trend. In Figure 7.3, you can see turning points at *D, E,* and *F* where this indicator worked very well. It also would have given a small profit at *G*.

However, the oscillator gives a false signal at both *A, B,* and *I,* as there is a trend in force at those points.

Take a closer look at the chart intervals *B − C* and *b − c.* The price rose from *b − c,* even as the oscillator registered a lower peak. This is another example of divergence between the indicator and the price, and (as with MACD) it can be a good signal that the price is about to reverse direction.

Conversely, note that the divergence at *I − J* and *i − j* is quite ambiguous due to the intervening "valley" in the Stochastic lines between *I − J.* This would need more confirmation from another indicator before becoming tradable.

Fibonacci Retracements

Fibonacci retracements are a totally different kind of indicator. They can provide uncannily accurate predictions of support

Figure 7.4   How Fibonacci Levels Predict Retracement Support and Resistance within a Range

and resistance *between* a given high and low (retracements within a trading range) as well as *beyond* it (extensions once a trend has launched).

Let's look at how retracement works in Figure 7.4.

The Fibonacci tool has been used to draw Fibonacci levels between *A – B* on the chart with levels of 23.6 percent, 38.2 percent, 50 percent, 61.8 percent (1 – 0.382), and 76.4 percent (1 – 0.236) defined by the user.

From point *B*, the price declines and then fails to rise above the 23.6 percent level, as noted on the chart. Despite one last-gasp spike, it falls to the 61.8 percent level and holds in that region. It fails to challenge the 38.2 percent level, then drops and touches 61.8 percent one last time before rising to form at double top with the original point *B*.

Note that the support at the 23.6 percent level failed to hold despite initial encouraging signs, which heralded another plunge. There was another battle at the 61.8 percent level (no chart notation) at the extreme right of the chart before the price collapsed again.

What happened after that? Let's examine Figure 7.5. In this chart, points *A* and *B* have been advanced so that what was previously point *B* is now *A*. (Point *B* was selected as the low prior to the price collapsing at the end of Figure 7.4.)

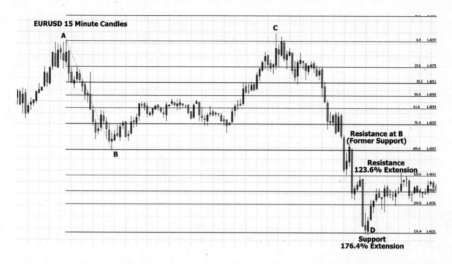

Figure 7.5   How Fibonacci Levels Predict the Extent of Breakouts

Once *B* was broken on the downside, it acted as resistance to a failed rally. The price then failed to hold at 123.6 percent as well and collapsed all the way to the 176.4 percent extension before rallying and holding at the 138.2 percent extension level.

If this example were to be continued further, points *C* and *D* would form the basis of a new Fibonacci level implementation, and the whole process would be repeated.

Note that the price followed Fibonacci levels quite accurately on this chart, but of course, this method is hardly foolproof. The biggest weak point is the ambiguity of when—and where—to shift the Fibonacci anchor points from which all the other levels are based.

Fibonacci levels require firm ground rules for when and where you anchor your drawing tool; otherwise, they are ultimately useless. After all, if you cannot establish a consistent methodology, then you cannot get consistent results, and you're unlikely to be successful as a FOREX trader. Your results must be repeatable.

Pivot Points

One potential way around the ambiguity of Fibonacci levels is the pivot point concept.

Pivot points can be calculated *automatically* on several trading platforms (either as a built-in function or an add-on), meaning that they can function as a far more objective indicator than Fibonacci levels.

The main pivot is neutral and is normally designated as P or PP. Any R level is considered a resistance level, any S level a support level, and any M level a midpoint between two others.

The M levels are numbered from the bottom up, and R and S levels are numbered outward from the P level.

The levels are determined by simple arithmetical formulas based on the previous day's high, low, and close.

$$P = (H + L + C)/3$$

Then,

$$R1 = (2*P) - L$$
$$R2 = P + (H - L)$$
$$R3 = H + 2*(P - L)$$

and

$$S1 = (2*P) - H$$
$$S2 = P - (H - L)$$
$$S3 = L - 2*(H - P)$$

The M levels are simply the midpoints of the other levels.

It's also possible to calculate weekly and monthly pivot points based on the previous week and month, but Figure 7.6 shows a selection of daily levels only. (The chart interval is the same as for Figure 7.5.)

The main focus of attention is the middle day. (You can see where the trading day changes—the pivot points are automatically recalculated and replotted by the software.)

The day starts at the neutral P level, where the price drifts and holds just below P before launching to $R1$, holding briefly at $M3$, and falling below P again. Previous support at P becomes resistance, and the price plunges vigorously to $M1$ (after a brief pause at $M2$

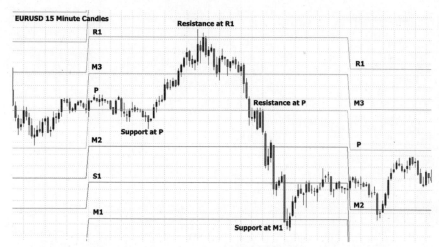

Figure 7.6   **How Pivot Points Can Help Determine Support and Resistance**

and *S*1). The price then finds support, rising to *S*1. The price falls again until arrested at *M*2, which has been replotted for the next day by the software.

While no method is infallible, pivot points are frequently very useful at determining where a given FOREX price will turn. As you can see, they are valid for both day trades and trades held overnight (but remember that the next day's pivot points can't be calculated until the close of the current day).

However, no indicator works best in isolation. For the best results, you need to combine several indicators to minimize the weaknesses of any one method.

Combining Several Indicators to Maximize Your Chances of Success

In Figure 7.7, several indicators have been plotted, including pivot points, a Stochastic oscillator, and a double-simple moving average (20 and 30 periods).

The best chances of a successful trade occur when more than one indicator work together to give solid buy and sell signals.

For example, the price dropped dramatically from *A* to *B*. Pivot point *M*1 provided solid support here; plus, note that the oscillator is in divergence with the price (it has made a higher low despite a new price low).

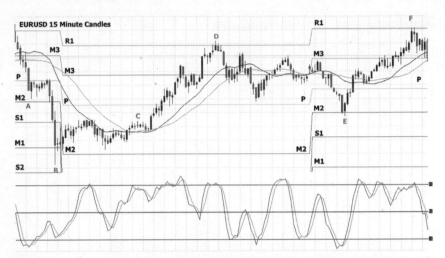

Figure 7.7 Trading FOREX Using Several Indicators: Pivot Points, a Stochastic Oscillator, and Moving Average Crossovers

Choosing to buy at *B* would have been a good choice, although you could have waited until *C* when the price fought its way over the moving averages (and the averages themselves soon crossed over afterward).

Point *D* was an excellent selling (or shorting) point, as divergence between the price and the stochastic oscillator appeared once more. Confirming this as a top was the fact that the price hit *R*1 while forming reversal candlesticks.

Your short sale from *D* could have been covered profitably at several points but especially once the price fell through to *E,* where it hit *M*2 (which had acted as support the previous day).

You could have bought once the price went over the moving averages again to run into *R*1 (which acted as resistance the previous day) at point *F.*

Of course, all these trades are hypothetical, and there is no real "system" defined here. But you *should* be able to see the advantages of using several indicators together to strengthen your convictions that the price will rise or fall.

It will take a fair amount of testing and trials to find something that fits the best with your own temperament and outlook. But by now, you should have some excellent ideas of how to begin experimenting to uncover a successful FOREX trading method.

Spot FOREX Alternatives: Other Ways to Profit from the FOREX Market

Most retail traders get involved with FOREX in one of two main ways: spot FOREX or currency futures.

There are also currency options to consider, and I'll discuss those, too, in just a moment.

So far, this chapter has discussed spot FOREX, as this particular market is unique to FOREX. Therefore, you should have a pretty good idea of how spot FOREX contracts work by now, including the difference between brokers and dealers and what you can expect from a spot FOREX trading platform.

But because this book already has a full section on futures, a basic discussion of futures instruments would be redundant in this chapter.

Instead, I'll compare and contrast spot FOREX to currency futures in Table 7.3 so that you can decide if currency futures are a better choice for your needs.

> **Note**
>
> Spot and futures contracts are frequently referred to as lots.

To make a long story short, spot FOREX is the better option if you're more interested in the following:

1. Short-term trading (i.e., day trading or swing trading, where you hold for a week or less)
2. Trading currency pairs, where the interest rate differential works in your favor and pays you money each daily rollover
3. Risking small amounts of capital until you know what you're doing

If you prefer longer-term trades and have a lot of capital to risk, you're better served by trading the futures contract for your favorite currency pair(s).

The Chicago Mercantile Exchange (CME) offered 49 futures and 32 options based on 20 currencies as of this writing, so you have

Table 7.3   Spot FOREX versus Currency Futures

Feature	Spot FOREX	Currency Futures
Trading Hours	24 hours a day, 5 days a week	Same as spot FOREX
Daily Downtime	Approximately 5 minutes a day for rollover	Approximately 30 minutes a day between the afternoon and evening sessions
Bid/Ask Spread	Usually set by the FOREX dealer (typically 2 pips on EURUSD and up from there)	Usually set by market forces on the exchange (smaller than spot spreads, on average)
Commission	Nonexistent on fixed spread accounts; otherwise, approximately $1/mini-lot each way	Approximately $5 per contract, round trip
Real Time Data	Free	Anywhere from $50 to $100/ month but includes noncurrency futures data
Trade Size Flexibility	Everything from micro-lots ($1,000 face value) up to mini-lots ($10,000 face value) and standard lots ($100,000 face value)	Micro-lots ($12,500) and mini-lots ($62,500) only on selected pairs; otherwise, full ($100,000) lots[a]
Rollover	Daily; can be a credit or a debit, depending on interest rate differentials	Infrequent, depending on how far out the contract expires
Transparency	Limited and uneven due to the decentralized interbank market	Regulated by centralized exchange rules
Ways to Trade	Fixed spread broker or commission-based ECN broker	Any standard futures account with a licensed futures broker
Ideal Trading Time Frame	Day trading or short-term trading (less than 2 weeks)	Longer-term trades lasting several days or weeks
Ideal Trading Size	Ideal for smaller traders just starting out	More suitable for larger and more experienced traders

Source: CME Group, "CME$INDEX Futures." Available at www.cmegroup.com.

roughly as many choices when trading futures as you do when trading spot FOREX.

Neither market is better than the other; they just serve slightly different purposes.

Why Trade Options Instead of Spot Contracts or Future Contracts?

Just like there are options on stocks, there are also options on FOREX, and they offer yet another way to profit on your analysis of where a given exchange rate will move.

There are two main types of FOREX options: the traditional call/put option (which functions just like a typical stock option; refer to Chapters 3 through 5 for various strategies) and also something called a "single payment option trading" contract.

Currency options (also known as FOREX options or just FX options) differ from futures in that you have the *right* to exchange money denominated in one currency into another currency at a preagreed exchange rate on a specified date. (Remember that a futures contract is an *obligation* to do the same thing.)

In return for purchasing the right to walk away from the trade if it's not in your favor, you pay an *option premium* for that privilege.

The worst that can happen in an options trade is that you lose 100 percent of the premium, plus whatever commission you paid to get into the trade.

In a spot FOREX or futures contract trade, your liability is potentially unlimited if the trade keeps moving against you.

Traditional, Basic Options Strategies

There are two main concepts behind trading currency options: profit making and hedging.

Profit-Making Strategy   In the case of profit making, you are trying to guess the correct size and direction of a price movement on or before a given date. Let's just go over the basic option play here for vernacular purposes. Please refer to Chapters 3 through 5 for more advanced options trading strategies.

So, say you decide that the euro is going up against the U.S. dollar in the next month. You could buy a call at (let's say) 1.4000 for one standard $100,000 lot, which expires at the end of that month. Your broker informs you that your premium is 10 pips ($100 for one standard lot).

Such an option is effectively a EUR call and a USD put simultaneously, as you are always long one currency and short another in any given currency pair. (If you had bought a EURUSD put, you would have bought a put on the euro and a call on the U.S. dollar.)

In one possibility for this example, the EURUSD rate never rises above the 1.4000 before your month is up, in which case it would expire worthless and you would lose only the premium you paid for it.

The other scenario is that the EURUSD rate rises above the 1.4000 rate, in which case you could take delivery of a standard lot at 1.4000 and sell it for a profit. If the EURUSD price rises to 1.4100, you would have 90 pips of profit (100 pips gross profit – 10 pips premium). This would be $900 for one standard lot.

Hedging Strategy   With the profit-making strategy, you are taking on risk to (hopefully) earn a reward. Hedging is just the opposite: You're reducing risk to *protect* a reward.

Let's say you don't want to exit an already-existing position in the futures or spot market yet. You're short one standard lot of the EURUSD pair in the futures market in a long-term trade.

You sold at 1.4000, and you have a good profit already at 1.3000. You expect a larger profit still (perhaps you feel it should fall to 1.150) before you need to roll over your futures contract or close out the trade.

However, you expect an upward surge in the EURUSD price against your position in the meantime. You don't want to be stopped out of the trade, but you want to protect your profit at 1.3000, too.

In that case, you would buy a currency option—specifically, a EURUSD call at 1.3000 for one standard lot (the same size as your existing futures trade). The expiration date should equal or exceed the duration of the expected run against you.

The profit on the call will equal your loss on your short futures position (less the premium you paid for the option). That way, you've protected yourself from an adverse run against your original short while staying in the trade.

Single Payment Options Trading (SPOT) Contracts and How to Use Them

Single payment options trading (SPOT) is a type of option product that allows you to set (1) the conditions that need to be met to receive a desired payout and (2) the size of the payout if those conditions are met.

In turn, a SPOT broker determines the likelihood that these conditions will be met and charges an appropriate option premium.

Single payment options trading contracts are also known as "binary options," because only two types of payouts are possible: You either collect the agreed-upon payout, or you lose your entire premium. Thus, a SPOT contract is a variation on a European-style option: You can't change your mind once you buy one, but you can convert your SPOT to cash when your agreed scenario occurs.

Let's say you believe that the EURUSD rate will break above 1.4000 within nine days. You would pay a certain premium to your broker and then collect the agreed payout in nine days if the EURUSD does in fact exceed 1.4000 within that time. However, if the EURUSD doesn't make it above 1.4000 before expiration, you lose the full premium.

Here are some common SPOT scenarios:

- *One-touch SPOT:* Pays out if the price touches a certain level. (It doesn't have to be at this level as the contract expires; it only needs to touch it.)
- *No-touch SPOT:* Just the opposite: It pays out if the price does *not* touch a certain level at any point.
- *Digital SPOT:* Pays out if the price is above or below a certain level.
- *Double one-touch SPOT:* Pays out if the price touches one of two set levels. You would take on such a bet if you feel the price is going to break out, but you aren't sure which direction it will go. (This is similar to a *long straddle* with standard options.)
- *Double no-touch SPOT:* Just the opposite: The market is in a range, and you feel it will stay that way. (This is similar to a *short straddle* with standard options.)

As you can see, you get flexibility with SPOT options that you can only get with fairly sophisticated standard options strategies. But the downside is that the premiums are generally higher than for standard options.

Please refer to Chapters 3 through 5 on options for a more extended discussion of options strategies.

Conclusion

In this chapter, I explained the role of the global FOREX market and where you as a retail trader fit into the bigger FOREX picture. I discussed the advantages FOREX holds over other markets (low transaction costs, unequalled liquidity, long trading hours, and exceptional leverage) and ensured that you now understand basic FOREX trading terminology.

We then covered the mechanics of spot FOREX contracts including rollover, plus the important fact that the FOREX market is less regulated than exchange-based markets. You are now aware of the software you should consider using to trade FOREX, as well as why you need to be wary of dealing desks offered by many retail dealers.

You should also know the difference between standard, mini-, and micro-lot FOREX accounts and why you should start your trading at the microlevel.

We even covered several of the most popular technical indicators used when trading FOREX, as well as the essential fundamental analysis you need to be aware of, even if you're a day trader.

Notes

1. Euromoney FX Poll 2008; the Euromoney FX survey is the largest global poll of foreign exchange service providers.
2. Bank for International Settlements, Triennial Central Bank Survey, December 2007.
3. World Federation of Exchanges, Annual Statistics 2007, Equity Markets.
4. Bank for International Settlements, Triennial Central Bank Survey, December 2007.
5. International Financial Services, London, "Foreign Exchange 2007," December 2007. Available at http://www.ifsl.org.uk/upload/CBS_Foreign_Exchange_ 2007.pdf.
6. Aite Group, "Retail FX Market: The Next Frontier," July 16, 2007. Available at http://www.aitegroup.com/reports/200707161.php.

CHAPTER

8

The Commodities Market

Commodities (Futures) Basics

Some say the commodities market is the last bastion of pure, free-market capitalism left in the world—a battleground in which your greatest enemy is yourself and the innate flaws of humankind that we all hold. Fear and greed are chastised, while success is marked by freedom from routine. The level of attainable triumph is capped only by the sky or intellectual blemish, whichever comes first.

Many of my professional peers have consisted of Yale grads and high school dropouts, former teachers and police officers, and have varied from fund managers to retail investors turned career traders. The fact that this business has drawn people from such differing walks of life is indicative of the necessary yet unique forms of proficiency and dexterity required to trade commodities. For that reason, the unlikely characters are often the ones who find success. Following his acceptance to Harvard Business School, famous hedge fund manager, and personal hero of mine, Paul Tudor Jones II said this of his decision to not attend: "This is crazy, because for what I'm doing here, they're not going to teach me anything. This skill set is not something that they teach in business school." With that in mind, I will use this chapter to share with you some of the knowledge I've learned through my colleagues' experiences, as well as the wisdoms obtained through my own missteps and conquests.

The commodity futures marketplace is a forum for price discovery that includes oil, gold, corn, lumber, copper, and many, many more. Essentially, it's a commodity if you can eat it, run your car with it, or if it hurts to drop it on your toe. Both speculators and commercial users are constantly bidding to buy and offering to sell these assets for delivery at a forward date. The relentless bartering is how the price of future capital is set. Now, only a small percentage of those trades are actually delivered, as speculative positions and hedges are typically covered before contract expiration. Commodities futures provide for a place where both capital-seeking returns can be risked and industrial users can mitigate their risks associated with price swings.

How and Where to Open an Online Account

Before you can buy or sell any commodities futures or options on futures, you have to set up a trading account. The process in and of itself is not complicated, but there are choices available for retail and career traders alike that didn't always exist. Derivatives exchanges are in a constant state of product development and innovation.

One of the single greatest advancements in futures trading came in 1992 when the Chicago Mercantile Exchange released Globex, the first electronic trading platform. Since Globex's debut, there have been several other platforms released, but the original electronic trading module has been globally dominant over its peers. It's used around the world and accounts for the majority of the online volume. Since the release of Globex, trading on the screen has reduced the need for brokers, but there are advantages to both that need to be considered when it comes time to set up your account.

Prior to the introduction of electronic trading, if you wanted to trade without using a broker, you would be forced to move to New York, Chicago, Kansas City, or another exchange city. From there, a seat would either need to be purchased or leased and elbows sharpened—and then off to the jungle that is the open outcry trading pits. Not only has screen trading allowed for broker-free trading in nonexchange cities, but it also allows you to basically go anywhere in the world with a laptop and Internet connection to trade commodities. That combined with near 24-hour trading for many commodities has truly globalized the industry.

Almost all markets, some more than others, are at least trending toward electronic trading. The screen continues to grab a larger and larger percentage of total volume traded, resulting in an outpacing of the open outcry pits when it comes to liquidity. That's because it's quicker, more efficient, and cheaper—not to mention that you also get immediate feedback on your trade in regard to fills, profits, and losses. There's no waiting for a broker's call and wondering why you did or didn't get an order in. Interactive Brokers has an excellent futures trading platform that is worth checking out.

Hedgers versus Speculators

There are many different types of market participants that use commodities futures markets. They come in all sorts of shapes and sizes and use the derivatives markets for a variety of different means. Those with vested interest in these markets can be classified into two basic groups: hedgers and speculators. The two broad categories of derivatives traders actually use commodities futures for opposite reasons but are completely dependent on one another in a sort of symbiosis to conduct their necessary business within the commodity futures marketplace.

A hedger is an individual or entity who uses commodity futures to mitigate price risk exposure. Hedgers typically consist of those with a commercial and/or industrial interest in a business related to a particular commodity. This could be a farmer, gold miner, grain elevator, oil driller, and so on. These commodity users either are producers, or they use the asset as an input cost. All have a vested interest, or curtain risk exposure, in the price action of the commodity they deal in; that is to say, unless they use the futures market to hedge that risk. The following is a look into how a corn farmer might use commodities derivatives to put on a hedge and significantly reduce or eliminate risk.

A hedge is based around the concept that cash and futures markets more or less move together and eventually converge. There are other aspects that come into play, such as changes in the basis (the price difference between the cash and futures markets) during the duration of the hedge, but for now, we'll simply look at an example of price movement unison between the cash and futures markets.

Without a hedge, a rise in the price of corn would benefit the farmer, and if the price fell, it would be a detriment. In other words, he or she has a long-side price exposure; hence, the farmer would implement what's called a long hedge. A short hedge is simply the opposite and might be conducted by a grain elevator that has to purchase grains on the cash market.

Going back to the farmer, imagine it's June, and the farmer is expecting to produce 50,000 bushels of corn at harvest. To put on a long hedge, he or she would sell 50,000 bushels, or short 10 corn futures contracts, on the forward markets. As the farmer harvests and sells his or her crop, he or she would in turn buy back his or her corn futures contracts and sell the crop on the cash market. The losses or gains in the futures contracts would offset the losses or gains related to the cash market exposure. Essentially, the farmer can secure the current cash market price, plus or minus the change in the basis over the hedge's lifetime, for a future date. Table 8.1 is an exact look at how this hedge would play out in both a rising and falling market.

There are several more hedging strategies, some of which are more complex than a simple long or short hedge, but the underlying premise is fairly consistent among them. Regardless, the futures market is necessary for farmers and other commercial users. Input prices, such as fuel, fertilizer, seed, and equipment costs are volatile and usually correlated with the price of the underlying commodity. The swings in input prices are significant indeed. It would be very

Table 8.1   Hedge Example

Long Hedge	Futures Market	Cash Market
June	Sell 10 Dec. futures contracts at $3.50/bushel	Current cash market exposure is a 50,000 bushels long position at a price of $3.50
Prices Rise		
November	Buy the Dec. futures contract back at $4.00	Sell inventory on the cash market at $4.00
Profit or Loss	$25,000 loss	$25,000 perceived profit
Prices Decline		
December	Buy the Dec. futures contract back at $3.00	Sell inventory on the cash market at $3.00
Profit or Loss	$25,000 gain	$25,000 perceived loss

difficult for commodities producers to stay in business without a futures market to hedge price risks, but hedgers only make up one side of the marketplace.

On the other side of the trades are the speculators. Speculators come in all sorts of shapes and sizes, consisting of the small retail trader who trades one and two contracts at a time to the hedge and investment funds who trade thousands. Specs often get a bad rap because of their ability to pile on and move markets off of equilibrium. Sometimes this is deserved, and other times they're just the easiest scapegoat.

Regardless, speculators are absolutely necessary to the commodity futures marketplace. As previously mentioned, hedgers use the marketplace to dissipate price risk exposures. Contrary to hedgers, specs use the futures markets to assume risk. They look to gain a return on their capital by risking it in the marketplace. This creates the previously mentioned symbiosis in which each entity, speculators and hedgers, is reliant on the other in order to conduct their desired business.

The best way to think about the relationship between hedgers and speculators is to compare it to an insurance policy. For this particular instance, we'll use a home fire insurance policy. The homeowner, who is the hedger equivalent, pays a premium to an insurance company, the speculator, in case the home catches fire. If the home never catches fire, the owner of the home paid the insurance policy for no other reason than peace of mind. The premiums he or she paid served no actual financial purpose. This is comparable to the previously mentioned scenario in which corn prices rose during the farmer's long hedge. Without the hedge, or the insurance policy, the farmer would have been better off and $25,000 richer. The other state of affairs consists of when corn prices fall—the house catching on fire. The insurance company is liable to pay for the damages caused by the fire. Both the farmer and the homeowner would be in a state of financial trouble relative to the size of the fire if they hadn't hedged their risk accordingly.

The relationship between the homeowner and the insurance company is extremely relative to that of the hedger and speculator. The main difference between the metaphor and the actual commodities market is that the speculators are constantly trading the insurance policies. With that given, the hedgers need the specs in order to mitigate their risk exposures. The speculators need the hedgers in order to gain a return on their capital risks. At the same time, each keeps the other honest. The two combined create a commodity futures marketplace—one in which proper bidding, offering, buying, and selling of tangible assets can result in an environment for proper price discovery to take place.

The Leverage Lion

I mentioned in the opening passage of this chapter that there is no place for fear when trading in commodities markets. I'm not saying that the pressures associated with an open position will be without anxiety and apprehension as well as adrenaline and anticipation. I'll be the first to tell you that it's a part of the business. As a commodities trader, you have to quell those emotions and separate them from the actual trading process. The moment your fervor takes over is precisely when you lose the ability to trade rationally and therefore successfully. This is the most frequent gaffe made by retail investors in the commodities space. The reasons for discussing these concepts have to do with one word that has come to carry mostly negative and fearful connotations: leverage.

Trading with leverage, whether it's buying options, using a double-long ETF, or trading on margin, tests the previously mentioned human emotions more intensely than, say, owning a mutual fund in your 401k that you may check monthly. But it's not simply just the tug-of war-played between fear and greed that we must battle while facing considerable short-term profits and losses.

Positions in levered products typically have a much shorter relative duration, forcing you to come face to face with those emotions on a regular basis. In other words, leverage creates a situation in which a small percentage of capital risked can have a large net percentage effect on a portfolio's value, while at the same time, it requires very active management. It's important to be aware of what to expect from yourself when trading on margin. One of my favorite adages in regard to trading is, "Leave your passion in the bedroom and your hope at church on Sundays." The bottom line is that leverage is not to be feared but respected. Only then will you be able to experience success in trading commodities markets.

Leverage has a reaching effect beyond that of you, the individual trader, and your portfolio. It has the ability to have rather significant short-term effects on the price of a commodity. This is a concept that is very important to be able to both comprehend and identify. In order to do just that, let's look at a few specific examples where this has occurred.

The first instance I want to mention is oil's notable run to nearly $150/barrel and the ensuing collapse below $30. We've already learned that neither one of these extremes was accurate, with the equilibrium falling somewhere between the two. So, how did we get there? The answer is a combination of speculators—mainly the big locals and investment funds—understanding public sentiment and public sentiment being mostly irrational during points of market extremes.

The economic climate during this period of market volatility was one that included a collapsing dollar with inflationary implications combined with massive recessionary forces. In other words, it was an environment of contradicting economic factors that is also referred to as stagflation. Now, while the dollar was falling and oil was spiking, the largely predominant public concern was inflation. With that in mind, the general public is often referred to as the dumb money, because they are typically the last ones in on a trade and the first ones to get burned. Famous trader Jesse Livermore once said, "Remember, the market is designed to fool most of the people most of the time."

Meanwhile, oil was pushing higher and higher, and the talking heads in the mainstream media were fearmongering; the large specs began to slam the long side of the market, putting more upside pressure on the market. This simply added fuel to the fire and was the perfect time for the dumb money to enter stage left with the mentality that oil will go up forever—a view that the public often holds during points of market extremes. This again added more bullish pressure and was accompanied by one last push of fund buying until the market topped out and turned. The sequence of events that took place in the price spike in light sweet crude oil was very typical of an overextended price run.

- Fundamentals turn the market bullish and are accompanied by light speculative buying, while the public sector and the media are typically completely unaware of the first price move.
- The large funds enter the market, often after a correction from the first leg, fueling the next big leg up.

- The dumb money enters the market using vehicles like ETFs as well as some derivatives products and adds more long-side pressure.
- The funds come in for the final push and blow the market out to the top side before it snaps back.

When you have such an extreme price run that takes place in this manor, as we did in the oil market, you can expect the correction to be rather violent. The higher they are, the harder they fall. Once the dollar and oil began to reverse trend, the public sentiment abandoned its inflation fear, while recessionary and deflationary panic grabbed a stranglehold. Talks of a second Great Depression started to become commonplace, and the specs took advantage of public fears, just as they did on the way up. As crude oil pushed lower, the funds hammered the short side of the market, timing their sales with key points of resistance.

The fact that the specs trade with leverage allows them to control much more capital than they actually have. This is what gives them the ability to push and pull markets during points of weakness. Being able to identify this concept is essential as a commodities trader. Avoid being the dumb money. The more you hear about a trade in the mainstream media, the more wary you should be of it. When your crazy uncle or the neighbor across the street tells you he or she is making the same trade, dump your position.

The last lesson to be taken from the price action in the crude oil market is that leverage accentuates the volatility of Adam Smith's concept of the invisible hand always pushing a market toward equilibrium. In the short run, leverage allows for the market to resist against the hand's pressure to correct the market. When crude shot past $140/barrel, the hand was pulling, and the leverage was pushing. Think of it like two people pushing on opposite sides of the door. When one person suddenly steps back, the other comes flying through. That's what happened as oil peaked and whipsawed back down. That occurs over and over again, with the market overshooting the equilibrium less and less with each passing until either the equilibrium has changed or the market is priced correctly.

This concept is extremely important to understand in this period of volatile economic and financial times. Don't just fade a trend because it's not trading where its fundamentals say it should be—even if it's way off. If your analysis is different from the market's price action, keep your position neutral until a new trend develops. Otherwise, you will become an indirect victim of a leveraged marketplace. John Maynard Keynes famously stated, "The market can stay irrational longer than you can stay solvent."

The $64,000 question becomes, how do you know when you're simply looking at leveraged market irrationality as opposed to a new fundamental trend? The answer lies within the Commodity Futures Trading Commission (CFTC). The CFTC releases a weekly report called the Commitment of Traders (COT). The COT report is a detailed look into the volume and open interest of a number of commodities traded on futures exchanges. This report is very handy, because it breaks down those statistics in a number of ways, including what percentage of the open positions are held by speculators versus commercial interests. Let's take a look at what this means and how one might analyze some of this data.

The soft winter wheat contract traded at the Chicago Board of Trade (CBOT) hit a significant bottom at approximately $4.25/ bushel during the first part of April 2007. Long contracts held by the noncommercial, or speculative, bottomed at 65,785 contracts in January, according to the January 16, 2007 COT report. Less than 11 months after the April bottom, the price of soft winter wheat had more than tripled and eventually peaked at $13/bushel in February. In January, the noncommercial longs hit their peak at 110,631 contracts, as told by the January 15, 2008 COT report. The ensuing collapse in wheat prices down to $4.50 in December 2008 was accompanied by a more than halving of spec longs, down to a level of 53,407 contracts reported in the December 2, 2008 COT report. Let's throw some statistics at these numbers to really show you the significant roll leverage played in the wheat market.

- At the market bottom, the cumulative spec long position was the equivalent of approximately 55 percent of the 2007/2008 U.S. soft winter wheat crop. At the peak, it was over 90 percent.
- In January 2007, the noncommercials managed approximately $1.4 billion of wheat on less than $180 million in margin. Leading up to the market top, the aggregate margins held by specs nearly doubled to approximately $350 million, while total crop value held had more than quadrupled to nearly $6.5 billion. Putting a ratio to that, for every dollar added in investment, $42.50 of wheat was procured.

- Remembering that most speculative positions are closed out prior to delivery date, the noncommercials covered their longs by selling approximately $5 billion worth of wheat on the futures market between the peak and December bottom.

Those are some fairly drastic figures, but they are a good representation of the power leverage can have on a marketplace. Ignorance of this concept is portfolio suicide, while knowledge of capital flows related to leveraged market is the ability to take advantage of volatile price swings such as those seen with the booms and busts of the wheat and oil markets. Combine that with the understanding that leveraged finance has the capability of clouding a clear trading mind with emotion. Remember, leverage is to be respected, not feared.

Commodities Trading Strategies

When it comes to trading commodities, differing strategies are a dime a dozen. The problem is that for every one good strategy, there are a hundred bad ones; and what may work for one trader often doesn't work for another. Regardless of whether you're a fundamentalist or technician, what it really comes down to is what works for you.

Spread trading, like the strategies outlined in Chapter 5, is an excellent way to play the commodities market. Spreads can be a great tool in allowing yourself exposure to commodities markets while at a risk level less than that of a naked long or short position. This notion is not to be understated, given today's highly volatile market climate. The idea of taking a net neutral position within positively correlated markets and trading price action and price spreads results in a more reduced risk-reward scenario than trading price action alone. Another benefit of using spreads is that your entry points don't have to be as precise as they would otherwise. Because of the highly leveraged nature of commodity futures, an entry point on a naked trade that is off by even a day or two can result in the trader getting blown out of a position before it gets a chance to move their way. Lastly, as a result of the reduced volatility, margin rates on spreads are typically lower than a simple long or short position, requiring less capital to trade.

The three previously mentioned traits of spreads can potentially be the difference between trading commodities comfortably and sitting on the sidelines. In fact, many career traders have made their living and experienced longevity, a rarity in this business, through the use of spreads. Contrary to popular belief, you don't have to be a pit trader or commodities guru to be able to employ these types of trading strategies.

Commodity spreads can be broken down into two main categories: intramarket and intermarket. An intermarket spread is comprised of a simultaneous long and short position of two or more futures contracts within different commodities markets. A few of the more commonly known and traded intermarket spreads include crude oil and reformulated gasoline (crack spread), natural gas and electricity (spark spread), and the gold-silver spread.

We are going to focus on the intramarket spread, which is typically an offsetting long and short position of futures contracts of the same commodity but different delivery months. For that reason, it's commonly referred to as a calendar spread. Intramarket trading is one of the simplest forms of spreading and one of the easiest ways to moderate risk exposure. I am of the opinion that this particular strategy is grossly underused by retail investors. The following is a look into the meat and potatoes of intramarket spreading.

When the price of a commodity moves either up or down, the delivery months closer to expiration, also called the front and/or near months, tend to experience a larger percentage move than the months with a delivery at a later date, the back months. This very important phenomenon is based around the fact that fundamentals such as supply, demand, inflation, economic climate, and so on are better understood and more predictable in the short run.

In other words, there are more unknowns in the long run, and the more severe a price trend is, the more pressure the market will be under to revert back to its historical mean. If a new historical mean is defined, which is typically a rare occurrence, the spot market almost always overaccentuates the first move and retraces some of the initial price action, which is why the back months lag in price action. In bringing this full circle, the cash market and front-month contracts represent the price discovery of current supply and demand fundamentals; the near-month contracts are priced with the expectation that market conditions will be fairly similar to the cash and front-month markets; and the back-month contracts epitomize the historically proven fact that nothing goes up or down in a straight line and that markets retrace.

Notes

In both the spirit of this book and the current market climate, there is something very important to note. I mentioned that throughout history, new historical means are rarely redefined. It has only happened a handful of times in the past 100 years. I fully believe we are in the middle of exactly one of those extraordinary times. The world economy is trying to redefine an equilibrium for liquidity, which has been represented by the violent shift from asset price inflation to asset price deflation. Which "-flation" is next is currently a highly debated topic. I'm not going to speculate on which will win out, but I do know that the adjusted monetary base is growing at near triple-digit annual rates, the Federal Reserve balance sheet has ballooned to multitrillion-dollar levels, and the U.S. government is running trillion-dollar budget deficits. This will absolutely result in a renewed volatility of asset prices. If history of finance and economics has proven one thing, it's that man has never been good at economic and market intervention. It's highly probable that these drastic steps undertaken by economic regulators amidst the greatest liquidity crisis in history will either over- or undershoot the proper equilibrium. This will redefine many historical price averages.

The light sweet crude oil futures market of 2008 and early 2009 was a perfect example of back–month contract prices being stickier than the near-month prices. During the record-setting price run in the oil market in the summer of 2008, the back-month contracts lagged and traded at a severe discount to the front-month contracts. A market in which the price of the commodity is more expensive in the front-month contracts than the back-month contracts is said to be in backwardation.

The oil futures market was a beast of a different nature at the beginning of 2009. After peaking above $140/barrel, we saw crude prices collapse to a $30/barrel handle. The price relationship of the oil futures contracts acted in a complete opposite manor to that seen in the summer spike. In this case, as markets collapsed, the back-month contracts traded at a significant premium to the spot price and front-month contracts.

This market climate, opposite to a market in backwardation, is referred to as being in contango. The notion to keep in mind here is that futures markets tend to approach or accentuate backwardation conditions during bull runs and do the exact opposite in moving toward a contango during bearish periods. I would like to briefly note that a market in contango is much more common to see in futures markets, because it has to discount both commodity storage costs as well as the risk-free rate of interest. That is why backwardation is named so. With that in mind, using intramarket spreads during the oil boom and bust were a very profitable yet more risk-averse way to trade the volatile crude market. Here's how the trades would have played out.

Let's say you developed a bullish bias toward light sweet crude oil in February 2007, and you wanted to trade this market using spreading techniques. First and foremost, it's important to note that the New York Mercantile Exchange (NYMEX) crude futures have a contract for every month of the current year and the five following years. This allows for a little more versatility in choosing which months to put your spread on. Given that it's February 2007 and you think the price of crude oil is going to rise, a possible intramarket spread would consist of buying the August 2007 contract and selling the January 2008 contract.

We'll use hypothetical but relative prices for this example: $63/barrel for the August contract, $65/barrel on the January contract, and a spot price of $60/barrel. Between February and July, the spot price of crude increased $20 to $80/barrel. Consistent with bull runs, the futures contracts started trending toward backwardation. The August contract increased by $16 to $79/barrel, while the January contract, which will represent a smaller percentage of the move in the spot price, increased only $15 and sits at a price of $80/barrel. At this point, or any other time during the spreads' lifetime, you will need to cover both your long and short contracts. This means you have to sell your August long back to the market for a profit of $16,000 per contract and cover your January short at a $15,000 loss per contract. Your net profit on this trade would have been $1,000 per spread.

Intramarket spreading with a bearish bias is simply conducted in the opposite manor: long the back month and short the near month. As the market sells off, the near-month contracts will lose more value relative to the back months. With a market in backwardation, such as the oil market pre-collapse, you're betting that the price spread will decrease. As we saw in the crude market, the price difference shrank until the price of the back-month contract surpassed that of the front-month contract. At that point, the market entered a contango, and the bearish calendar spread is now profitable when the spread difference grows.

There are a couple of things to note in closing about intramarket trading. Although calendar spreads reduce risk exposure, it allows for entry-point leeway, and has reduced margin rates, remember that you're still dealing in levered products. The longer and further a commodity moves from its historical norm, the more extreme the price divergence among the futures contracts will be. This will result in a more severe contango or backwardation, which means more volatility and risk involved in the spread. Given that, intramarket spreads are a great tool to give your portfolio the necessary exposure to commodities market. Remember, risk can never be eliminated, but it can be managed.

Volatility Revisited

Using options on commodities futures can be a very beneficial tool when utilized properly. They allow for a vast addition of different strategies that would be limited by otherwise trading futures. However, as stated earlier in this book, the volatility effect when trading options is often overlooked by novice traders. I cannot stress the importance of volatility enough; so, let's take a more in-depth look at volatility, but this time in terms of commodities.

Volatility is the velocity and magnitude of futures price movements, regardless of the direction. In options, volatility is given a numerical value as a percentage that is really just a measure of risk. Using gold for an example, let's say that volatility on gold futures is currently 10 percent. Ten percent is equal to a 1 standard deviation price move on an annualized basis. For example, on January 1, the gold futures contract is trading at 900. On December 31, with the 10 percent volatility, you could have expected the price of gold to range between 810 $(900 - 900 \times 10\%)$ and 990 $(900 + 900 \times 10\%)$ approximately 68 percent of the time. The other 32 percent of the time, the price would have been outside that range: 16 percent of the time above and 16 percent below. This is based on a normal probability distribution in which observations that fall within a range of plus or minus 1 standard deviation from the mean are equal to 68 percent of the total observations. Figure 8.1 is a visual of this concept.

For the sake of this piece, we will use the figures in the normal distribution, but it isn't the most accurate probability distribution

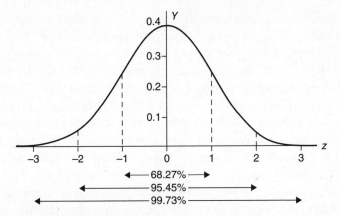

Figure 8.1 Probability Distribution

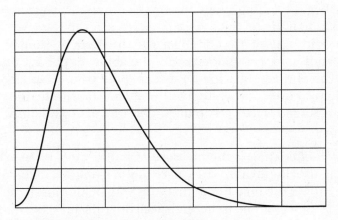

Figure 8.2 Commodity Skew Distribution

that we can use. Most statistically random events that have zero as the lower limit, such as futures trading, follow a log-normal distribution.

As you can see, the graph in Figure 8.2 is skewed to the right. This has the effect of slightly raising the percentage of observations that fall within 1 standard deviation. It also means that the probability of the price dropping in half is equal to the probability of the price doubling. Using our gold model, the chance of gold futures dropping to 450 is equal to the probability of the price of gold going to 1,800. This is the distribution that most options pricing models, including the Black-Scholes model, use for their computations.

Regardless, each commodity has its own distribution that can be computed by plugging in price data points, but most will closely follow the log-normal distribution.

The differences between a commodity's actual distribution and the log-normal distribution are represented in the premiums given by options traders to different strike prices. This is called the volatility skew and is a discussion in and of itself. All you need to know for now is that the further a strike price is from the futures price, the more skewed it will be. There are a few different theories for this, but it's probably due in large part to the lottery effect. This is the notion that people are willing to bet on the chance to win big. The lottery gives you terrible odds on your money, but the prospect of hitting the jackpot keeps people coming back. It's no different with far-out-of-the-money options.

The beautiful thing about trading volatility is that you don't necessarily have to trade price direction. In fact, you can trade volatility as a commodity by itself. Combining a good fundamental and technical understanding of a commodity with the ability to predict the direction of volatility can be a great way to expose yourself to large price moves in your direction while grossly reducing downside risks. Before going on, let me briefly recap the different types of volatility:

Historical volatility is the measure of past futures price action. It is usually measured in a 20-day moving average. You can choose the time frame that suits you, but it must have at least 20 observations to be statistically significant. Historical volatility can be helpful to measure actual volatility but should not be used to predict it.

Implied volatility is the market's estimate on how volatile the futures market will be from the current date until the contract expires. This is extremely difficult and tedious to compute by hand, as it requires working backwards through the pricing models, but there is plenty of different software available that will easily compute this for you.

Actual volatility is a measure on how much futures *will* change between now and expiration. This is what we're trying to figure out in order to figure out when you're getting a good deal on an option or when you're not.

Let's regroup here and take a look at two examples using our gold futures contract to see exactly how volatility can be traded.

Example 1: Implied volatility is currently 20 percent, and you believe actual volatility is going to be 30 percent (again, meaning the market thinks volatility will be 20 percent from now until expiration, but *you* think it will be 30 percent). If you were bullish on price action, you buy a call. A bearish stance would require you to buy a put. You would buy both the put and call (see "Straddle Strategy" in Chapter 5) if you were neutral on the market outlook. All three strategies result in a long volatility position.

Example 2: Let's say you're bearish on volatility and expect it to drop from 30 percent to 20 percent. If you are bullish on gold prices, you would sell a put. If you think prices will drop, the trade is to short the call. A market neutral position calls for you to sell both the call and the put. These positions are short premium.

As you can see from this example, you don't necessarily have to pick which way the market is going to move. You can strictly trade volatility by simply going short or long premiums. Regardless of whether you have a position on price action, you should always implement volatility in your trades. Let's say your views on actual volatility are correct, and you do take a long or short stance on prices. If the market moves against you, your losses will be limited, because volatility moved in your favor. Positions in which you get both volatility and price direction correct turn out to be big winners and sometimes multipliers. Trading volatility simply makes for a much more favorable risk-reward scenario.

This all seems really great, but I've taken one extremely large liberty up to this point. How do we figure out which way volatility is going? That is obviously a very important question. It's definitely imperative, given today's economic climate, to keep an eye on such things as geopolitical issues, new financial regulation, and monetary/fiscal happenings. Also, curtain commodities have specific seasonal tendencies. Grains are most volatile during growing periods in the summer. Orange juice is volatile in the winter and during hurricane season. Live cattle tends to have an increase in volatility as contracts close on expiration, while the eurodollar increases in volatility until the futures become near-month contracts. With that in mind, I have something else for you that will be of benefit when trying to figure out the direction of volatility.

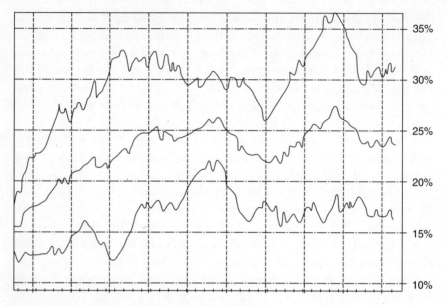

Figure 8.3   Central Tendency of Volatility

I'm referring to a concept called the central tendency of volatility. The central tendency of volatility is just the historical volatility of a futures contract through its lifespan. To compute the central tendency, you start by calculating the monthly historical volatility. So, instead of having a 20-day moving average, you'll have a 20-month moving average. You then take those figures and log them with the corresponding month and the corresponding contract through the prior years.

The central tendency gives you the point at which half of the time volatility was above, and which half of the time it was below. Then, just as you did at the very beginning of this section, find the standard deviation of the central tendency, and what you have is the volatility of volatility. In other words, 68 percent of the time, the volatility of your futures contract will fall within plus or minus 1 standard deviation of the central tendency. Figure 8.3 is a chart of the central tendency of volatility and a brief example of how to use it.

The middle line is the central tendency, while the top and bottom lines account for the standard deviations. Let's say volatility is trading at or near the bottom line. Statistically, we can assume that there is an 84 percent (68% + 16%) chance that volatility will be higher than its current value. At this point, you would want to get long volatility with one of the previously mentioned strategies. If volatility was trading at the top, you would do the opposite and short premium.

Using volatility in options is much like playing poker. A good poker player gives himself or herself a statistical advantage over the bad players. When he or she puts his or her money in the pot, he or she has a better chance to win than the poor player. He or she will have bad beats and get sucked out on the river, but more often than not, he or she will take the pot. In the long run, he or she will be a winner. If you think the gold market is going to go up, you can go long price and can also either sell or buy premium, and vice versa. Being on the right side of volatility is the equivalent of being the better poker player. If you put yourself in a position to be successful, you will.

Conclusion

In this chapter, we examined the commodities market. We went over the difference between hedgers and speculators and how these two different types of traders affect commodities prices. We tackled leverage and its dominant force in the commodities markets. Last but not least, we took another look at volatility and how it is important when trading options on futures, or any other market, for that matter.

The futures market is a very exciting market to trade in. Then when you throw options into the mix, the game gets very intense. You can employ all of the options strategies I talked about in Chapters 3 through 6 to any commodity you deem fit.

Single Stock Futures: A New Form for Derivative Investing

Single Stock Futures have always been a bit of an enigma to traders in the United States, regardless of their relative popularity overseas. Disallowed on U.S. exchanges in the 1980's because no one could decide which government agency would oversee regulation, Single Stock Futures made a comeback in late 2002 and has been gaining popularity ever since.

Some say this is the burgeoning market of the future—other's say that it's doomed to fail. This chapter will give you all the information you need to make that decision for yourself.

What Are Single Stock Futures, and Where Are They Traded?

To the dismay of many, financial markets are often irrational. This may be the result of any number of factors, including government intervention, monetary policies, excessive speculation, or shear mob mentality. Gordon Gekko memorably claimed in the 1987 film *Wall Street*, "You're walking around blind without a cane, pal. A fool and his money are lucky enough to get together in the first place."

Although it was just a movie about insider trading, the quote holds many truths. In Chapter 8 on commodities, a reference was made to the notion that markets behave in a way that hurts most participants most of the time. If that's the case, then wouldn't the general public be the irrational ones, while the marketplace is either rational or a logical representation of mass public irrationality?

The last thing I want to do here is give a philosophical lecture on sensible reasoning, and for the sake of this chapter, the answer to that question is neither here nor there. The point is that whether a market is irrational or is just perceived as such is irrelevant. Finance is all about figuring out what the price of an asset should be and being able to buy below or sell above that price.

Market irrationality, which again is relative, creates unwarranted price action. This creates opportunity for the investors. The point is that instead of fighting it, embrace and profit from these occasions. Markets with greater obscurity that trade less volume and have more complex pricing models will result in more frequent deviations of asset valuations from their equilibriums. Some extreme examples of this are mortgage-backed securities and credit default swaps (CDS). A significantly less dramatic case is the market for single stock futures. This chapter will take a look into everything from the history and basics of these derivatives contracts to more complex pricing models and trading strategies.

Single stock futures are an agreement between a buyer and a seller to deliver a securities product at a forward date and with a predefined price. The contract size is 100 shares for stocks, while ETFs can be traded in blocks of 100 or 1,000. The listed underlying securities are some of the most frequently traded equities and ETFs. Expiration dates of the contracts are the third Friday of each delivery month. There are some similarities between single stock futures and other derivatives products.

Single stock futures are traded on margin, usually equivalent to 20 percent (both initial and maintenance) of the value on the contract. This rate is recomputed daily as the stock price changes and should be watched accordingly as to avoid a margin call. It is also subject to your particular brokerage house. Options spreads (refer to Chapter 5) can be used to both lower premiums and lower your risk exposure. The main difference between single stock futures and other futures markets is the percentage of deliveries taken. Only about 5 percent of commodities or equities index futures are delivered. Single stock futures have a delivery rate of approximately 95 percent.

This debunked one of the chief motives against having a single stock futures market. There was a belief that this securities derivatives product would take volume and liquidity away from the cash market. A similar conviction was held prior to implementing a futures market for U.S. Treasury notes. The large percentage of deliveries taken contributed to proving those worries unjustifiable. Liquidity actually increased as a result of adding the derivatives product.

If you've never heard of single stock futures, don't worry. They have a rather unique history. On December 21, 2000, former president Bill Clinton signed into law the Commodity Futures Modernization Act of 2000. Part of the legislation included a repeal of the Shad-Johnson Accord, which banned trading of single stock futures. They weren't banned because of an issue relating to the price discovery process or extreme speculation. Single stock futures are a combination of a derivative and a securities product. The Securities and Exchange Commission and the Commodity Futures Trading Commission couldn't agree on which body is to regulate these hybrid investment vehicles. The Shad-Johnson Accord was supposed to be temporary, but it obviously wasn't. Regardless, on November 8, 2002, single stock futures resumed trading.

Notes

This is just another example proving that the complete failure of the bureaucratic process in the United States is nothing new. The ego and power struggle of regulators in the 1980s seems to hold many resemblances to what we're currently seeing between the SEC chairwoman Mary Schapiro and U.S. Secretary of the Treasury Tim Geithner. I would postulate that similar to the Shad-Johnson Accord and Sarbanes-Oxley, the current overhaul of financial regulations in the United States will result in near utter failure.

The only exchange in the United States that currently offers trading of single stock futures is OneChicago. Like the IntercontinentalExchange (ICE), OneChicago does not have open outcry trading pits. All single stock derivatives are traded electronically, requiring a front-end setup through your brokerage firm. With that in mind, a single stock futures exchange, combined with the cash and stock options market, means that investors now have more options available to them. There are advantages and disadvantages to each investment vehicle. Let's look at how single stock derivatives compare to the other two securities-based markets.

I previously mentioned that margin requirements on single stock futures are approximately 20 percent. That is significantly less than what the typical requirements for a margin loan on your stock account would be. Buying cash market stocks on margin typically has an approximate requirement of 50 percent, alongside a very high rate of interest. This means that you have more leverage available to you with the futures market. Another significant advantage of using single stock futures is that they are exempt from short-selling restrictions such as the uptick rule. On the other hand, a holder of single stock futures does not have shareholder rights. I also want to briefly mention that trading halts in the cash market carry over to the futures market.

There are also discrepancies between the futures and options markets. As with any derivatives product, an option is the right but not the obligation to take delivery of the underlying security. Also, an option contract can expire out of the money and worthless, resulting in a loss of the premium paid. There are no such worries with futures. You must have a reasonably sound understanding of mathematics in order to maximize potential successes as an option trader. Not being able to quantitatively analyze an option's value is like swimming upstream. Understanding volatility and the value it takes in the price of an option is a near must. The similarities and differences between the three markets are important to know and understand, but I did not mention the most vital irregularity.

Holders of a long position in a single stock future do not receive any dividend payouts. On the other side of the trade, short sellers are also not liable to distribute any dividends. This has to be priced into the futures contract in the form of a discount. Not only do traders have to figure out future stock valuation, but they also have to quantify the value and risks associated with a potential change in dividend payouts. This complicates fair-value calculations and is the market irrationality referred to in the opening paragraphs that leads to the unique opportunities in trading single stock futures.

An arbitrage opportunity is a trade that has no risk, with a return above the risk-free rate of interest. They're generally extremely rare in financial markets. As an example, we'll look at an arbitrage opportunity in a market other than single stock futures. Let's say

Commodity Exchange (COMEX) Gold in New York is trading at $900 per ounce, while gold on the London Metals Exchange (LME) is trading for $905 per ounce. Me, and everybody else who noticed the discrepancy, would be racing to our trading platforms to buy as much COMEX gold as we could while simultaneously selling an equal amount of gold on the LME. For every New York–London spread put on, I would make $5/ounce.

Given the instantaneous access to global markets via electronic trading, the price divergence would first of all probably not exist, but if a riff did form, it would be closed in a matter of seconds. Think about my long New York–short London spread multiplied by thousands of traders and tens of thousands of futures contracts. The buy-side pressure would lift COMEX prices and the short sellers would knock down LME prices until the two markets converged. The absence of arbitrage in single stock futures is much less definitive.

Market participants can't look at single stock futures and as readily tell if an arbitrage opportunity exists. The gold trade was a no-brainer, where the only thing to note was the price difference between the two contracts. It wasn't as if gold on the COMEX had a dividend and LME gold didn't.

Single stock futures traders have the task of quantifying the value, or value lost, by the absence of a dividend. In other words, the fact that single stock futures traders have to trade price action on top of dividend expectations results in a more extensive and hazy price discovery process.

As a consequence, it's more common with single stock futures than other derivatives markets to see contracts stray from fair valuation. Any time a market, regardless of asset class, is trading at a price different from its true valuation, an opportunity presents itself. Being able to recognize an arbitrage prospect can potentially lead to extremely low-risk profit scoops. This concept will be revisited in much greater detail later throughout the chapter.

How to Trade and Value Single Stock Futures

One of the most important aspects to trading any asset is finding a proper valuation. If you're able to do that, the trading is fairly simple. Buy below fair value, and sell above fair value. If your calculations prove to be correct, you'll make money.

The following equations displayed are a couple of different looks representing how to assess present value for single stock futures. As mentioned in the beginning of this chapter, this is a little more complicated than assessing the value of corn or oil. At first look, fair-value calculations appear a little messy, but I will give you a few different looks at the equations and provide explanations and examples on how to use them.

If a company with a single stock future listing does not have a dividend, fair value is simply computed by the following equation:

$$SSF = SP * e \wedge r[(T_x - T_0)/360]$$

The previously mentioned equation will be the same for any commodity derivative. All you have to do is replace the stock price with the cash market price for the commodity. The discrepancy between valuing single stock futures and commodity futures lies within the dividend. The fair-value equation for a single stock future with a dividend follows:

$$SSF = SP * e \wedge r[(T_x - T_0)/360] - D * e \wedge r[(T_x - T_D)/360]$$

The variables in these fair-value equations are as follows:
  SSF = fair value for the single stock future
  SP = current stock price
  D = dividend yield
  T_x = time until expiration
  T_0 = date of evaluation
  T_D = date of dividend distribution
  r = net risk-free rate of interest (yield on a Treasury bill or savings account)
  e = mathematical constant and irrational number (2.71828 ...) that is used in compound interest equations

Let's go through an example using these formulas. Stock XYZ is currently trading at $100 a share and does not have a dividend yield. The current yield on a treasury bill is 3 percent, and there are 90 days until expiration. Without a dividend, we can use the first equation:

$$SSF = (100) * e \wedge 0.03[(90 - 0)/360] \approx \$100.75$$

The fair value for XYZ is approximately $100.75. In other words, using the compounded risk-free rate of interest to compute present value puts a premium into the price of the single stock future's contract. The premium is equated into the price, but forward earnings and other market circumstances will also be priced in.

Remember that futures contracts are an agreement between a buyer and seller for delivery at a specified forward date. The price discovery process is a representation of the market participants' forward-looking expectations on earnings, including the risk-free interest rate premium, on the share value of XYZ.

If you're having trouble grasping this concept, there is a more intuitive way to understand present-value calculations. In the world of theoretical economics and finance—a dangerous world that eliminates many outside factors and should be used carefully—the risk-free rate of interest is equal to or fluctuates infinitesimally around expected inflation. This result is an extension from theories on long-run lending. The banking sector will lend at rates slightly above the London Interbank Offered Rate (LIBOR), which is the interest rate at which banks can borrow unsecured funds from other banks.

The LIBOR typically tracks the Federal funds rate, which in turn is the usual basis for yields on Treasury bills. Long-run macroeconomic theory conjectures that lending is a zero-profit game. In a pure free market, lenders will enter the market and continually undercut the competition until the firms on the margin are lending at a rate equivalent to the rate they pay to borrow money (LIBOR). Still, in hypothetical land, the margin lender will require the firms lending above the LIBOR rate to reduce the interest rates they offer in order to receive business, and the banks who can't afford to lend at those levels will be eliminated.

Let's look at this in a theoretical example, keeping these relationships in mind:

Expected inflation = currency's change in purchasing power

$\qquad$ = LIBOR = federal funds rate

$\qquad$ = yield on a U.S. Treasury note

$\qquad$ = banks' lending rates

Example: Let's say a bank lends $10,000 at a rate of 5 percent interest over the life of the loan. The borrower will pay the bank $10,500. The expected inflation rate, which equals the loan's interest rate, will result in a 5 percent decline in the dollar's purchasing power. In other words, the $10,000 at point *A* can buy the same amount of a basket of goods, which is now 5 percent more expensive, as the $10,500 at point *B*. The nominal return for the bank is $500, but the real, inflation-adjusted return is zero.

We can relate that exact concept to our example of the single stock futures for Company XYZ. Every time you buy an asset, you are essentially borrowing money from yourself. The opportunity cost of tying up that money is the risk-free rate of interest, meaning the long-side traders can make 75 cents, in present value, for every $100 they invest risk free.

The traders selling the contract short are expecting *inflation* to be 75 cents a share, again using present value, and require relative premium for loss in purchasing power. Fair value simply tells us that the real return of an XYZ futures contract will be zero if the future expires at $100.75. One last note: Changes in expected inflation will result in changes of the premium value defined in the fair-value calculation. This will be looked into on a more in-depth level in the next section.

Stepping away from macroeconomic theory, let's add into the fair-value equation a dividend yield of $4 a share that will be distributed in 45 days. The computation is as follows:

$$\text{SSF} = (100) * e \wedge 0.03[(90-0)/360] - 4 * e \wedge 0.02[(90-45)/360]$$
$$\approx \$100.75 - \$4.01 \approx \$96.74$$

As a result of not receiving dividends while holding a single stock futures contract, the fair value declined when a dividend was introduced. I mentioned in the first section of this chapter that dividends aren't collected by the longs or paid out by the shorts.

Essentially, a dividend requires a discount to be priced into the single stock future value. A trader looking to go long will not be willing to pay as much for shares of stock he or she won't be receiving a dividend on. On the flip side of the trade, the short seller doesn't have to pay out dividends; therefore, he or she will be willing to sell the stocks short at a discounted rate.

The concepts in this section are very important to understand for any type of investing. Single stock futures in which the underlying company issues a dividend simply add a tweak to the calculations and another aspect to consider when trading. The following section will discuss how using single stock futures can significantly add to the versatility of your portfolio.

Using Single Stock Futures to Diversify Your Portfolio

Single stock futures are practical and convenient in a number of different ways when it comes to hedging your portfolio. The first aspect to note is the ease of trading these contracts short. This was discussed in the opening chapter, but it's worth mentioning again, being it has significant value. Sticking with our favorite imaginary company, assume that an investor owns 1,000 shares of Company XYZ. They have recently turned bearish, but the problem is that XYZ is set to distribute a dividend payment in two months' time.

Without single stock futures, the trader would be forced to try to quantify the downside risk using his or her tools of fundamental and technical analysis. After that, the figure would be compared to the dividend yield, and a decision to hold or sell would be made regarding the profitability of the potential circumstances.

Single stock futures give the investor the liberty to avoid that decision. Selling 10 XYZ futures against the 1,000 share position will hedge the trader from downside risks. The trader now has a neutral position: long 1,000 shares of XYZ in the cash market and short 1,000 shares of XYZ in the futures market. The following is an example of how hedging can be beneficial to your portfolio.

Assume XYZ is trading at $100 per share and is set to pay a dividend of $3 per share, and your analysis turned out correct, as the stock eventually dropped to $95. Your long cash market position experienced a loss of $5,000 but was offset by a $5,000 gain on your futures position. The initial 1,000 shares in your portfolio are used to deliver the 1,000 shares sold short on your futures position. You no longer own any shares of XYZ but in the process collected $3,000 of dividend payouts, which is the profit of this trade.

Without a hedge, your analysis would have told you that the downside risk in the stock outweighs the dividend yield, and you would have exited your position. That's $3,000 you would have missed out on.

As a brief example, let's just say the dividend will actually pay out $6 per share, and the other factors are the same. In the non-hedged scenario, you would have held your cash market position until the dividend payout. Your net profit would have been $1,000 ($6,000 − $5,000), which still falls well short of the $6,000 profit that could have been made using single stock futures to hedge.

What if your forecasts for XYZ had turned out to be wrong, and the share price rallied to $105? If you had a hedge on, it doesn't matter whether your views turn out right. The gains would be realized on the cash market position, while your futures position would incur the losses. The end result would still be a net of $3,000. Had you not hedged your shares of XYZ or hedged half of your position, your profits would have been $8,000 or $5,500, respectively. That is where the risk, for lack of a better word, in using a hedge lies.

Now, those of you who have been paying close attention are probably saying, "Wait a second here. Didn't you say in the prior section that fair-value pricing is accounted for and discounted in the price of the stock's futures contract? Shouldn't that nullify the potential benefits of hedging a cash market position with a futures market position?" The answer is both yes and no.

I discussed in the first section of this chapter the notion of arbitrage. That's what we're looking at here. Theoretically, a hedge of this nature shouldn't be profitable. There's a very long mathematical proof called the nonarbitrage condition that attests that neither an economic or financial equilibrium can exist when arbitrage is present. Lucky for us, we don't live in a textbook, and markets often deviate from their equilibrium.

I will admit that a hedge using single stock futures isn't as cut and dry as perceived by the previously mentioned example. It's still possible to implement a hedge to take advantage of dividends; you just have to consider some of the concepts already mentioned in this chapter.

Let's get back to Company XYZ, but this time, we'll use fair-value assessment and the following figures:

$SP = 100$

$D = 3$

$T_x = 60$

$T_D = 60$

$T_0 = 0$

$r = 4$ percent

The perceived fair value you pay for holding the stock is $100.67, and the fair value for the dividend is $3.02. All other things equal, subtracting the two gives us a futures price for XYZ of $97.65. Unfortunately, this theoretical future price has no directional bias, which almost never happens.

In other words, all things are not treated. If the market is bullish, the futures price will be trading above $97.65, and vice versa. Without using the present value of our figures, we could simply say that the breakeven point for a hedge would be the current stock price minus the dividend yield; a breakeven hedge for XYZ would be $97. Selling a future anywhere above that point will lock in profits.

Now, we need to add present value into our little equation to define the breakeven point for hedging your stocks. The magic number is equal to the stock price minus the dividend plus the opportunity cost of tying up your capital:

$$\text{Breakeven point} = SP - D + R * SP + R * (\text{margin rate}) * SP$$

$$R = r * [(T_x - T_0)/360]$$

In our case, the equation will yield the following:

$$100 - 3 + (0.0067) * 100 + (0.0067) * (0.20) * 100 \approx 97.80$$

If you sell the XYZ futures against your portfolio at a price of $97.80, your net will be zero. Any hedge above $97.80 is an arbitrage trade in which the profits are equal to the number of shares multiplied by the difference between the breakeven point and your hedge.

For example, if we hedged at $98.50, our *real return* would be $700, while the nominal return would be $1,500. Keep in mind that the breakeven point was calculated with 60 days until expiration. The chart in Table 9.1 is a representation of how this figure changes

Table 9.1   Breakeven Points

Days until Expiration	Breakeven Point
30	97.40
40	97.53
50	97.67
60	97.80
70	97.93
80	98.07
90	98.20
100	98.33
110	98.47
120	98.60

relative to changes in expiration.[1] All other factors are treated as constant.

The point is that these figures can be computed with relative ease at any point during the period you hold the stock. There will most likely be a number of different times in which the price of the futures contract is trading above the breakeven point. Your particular hedge can be set up a contract or two at a time.

A partial hedge that leaves part of your cash position naked can also be used. All that's required is a little tweak to the breakeven point equations, and you can compute a new magic number. Arbitrage trading is a rather foreign notion to many. It starts with an understanding of the concepts, followed by a little practice. You're well on your way.

Risks Associated with Single Stock Futures

The opening passage in this chapter talked about how assets stray from equilibrium prices as a result of either irrational markets or an irrational public perception. Don't misunderstand me when I state this, but the last two sections of this chapter have looked at theoretical valuations and in doing so have taken several things for granted.

All of the concepts discussed are extremely important to understand, but we must be careful with the assumptions. We used several economic statistics and statistical relationships within our fair-value equation. Unfortunately—or fortunately, as I should say—many of those correlations aren't true in the current economic climate.

This makes it even more difficult for the market to properly price the single stock futures contracts. The reccurring theme of this chapter has been that as price discovery becomes more muddled, assets stray more frequently and further from their equilibriums. The greatest risk is also our greatest opportunity. To understand the former is to realize the latter.

We previously discussed that the ability to earn a risk-free rate of interest results in a premium paid on the price of a single stock future. The notion is based around the theoretical relationship between interest rates and inflation—that being that the two are equal.

Our current economic climate has resulted in the previously mentioned statement being completely false. The following figures are the current (August 14, 2009) figures that are assumed to be equal in the second section of this chapter. As you will see, these statistics are anything but equal. I'll explain economically how that can happen, and then we'll look at how this affects the market for single stock futures.

LIBOR rate: 1.51 percent

Treasury yield: 0.41 percent

Federal funds rate: 0.15 percent

CPI: 3.4 percent[2]

30-year fixed mortgage rate: 5.38 percent

The consequences of this severe divergence among these rates can be boiled into a one-word description: imbalance. The fact of the matter is that the market for lending is not a pure free market. There are free-market aspects that affect lending rates, but that is not the driving force.

In actuality, the Federal Reserve has a monopoly on the price of money (interest rates). The two main tools they use to control, or try to control, interest rates are the federal funds rate and asset purchases.

The federal funds target rate is the overnight lending rate used by U.S. institutions. It's used to either stimulate economic growth by lowering it or to reign in excessive expansion by raising it. Right now, they are currently conducting an extremely aggressive expansionary policy. An interest rate is called negative real when inflation is greater than the rate, and there's no rule that says the Fed can't reduce the federal funds rate to negative real numbers.

That's exactly the situation with the CPI grossly outpacing the official overnight lending rates. Recall back to the second section and the bank lending example. We stated that inflation and the lending rates were even, and the net profit of the bank was zero. If the bank lent at a rate of interest less than inflation, they would lose money. The bank, unlike the Fed, has to report earnings and is exactly why the mortgage rate is significantly higher than the federal funds rate.

The second tool the Fed uses is its asset purchasing programs—like the failed Troubled Asset Relief Program. Lending rates are basically dependent on three main factors: inflation, supply and demand, and the secondary lending market. We've already discussed the effects of inflation. Interest rates, like any other asset, are largely affected by supply and demand. Figure 9.1 shows the market for loanable funds.

Interest rates increase when the supply of funds declines and/ or the demand increases, and vice versa. As banks have incurred losses and battled solvency, they have lacked the ability to both make new loans and purchase mortgages on the secondary market. At the same time, demand for loans has increased. This has contributed to mortgage rates outpacing inflation.

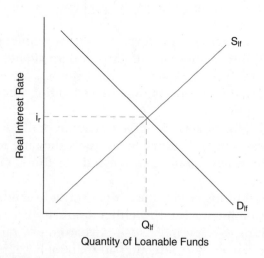

Figure 9.1   Market for Loanable Funds

In order to combat rates climbing too high, the Fed has been active on two different fronts. The first has to do with the previously mentioned federal funds rate. By giving banks access to cheaper overnight rates, they have been able to make more loans than would otherwise be possible. The second involves the secondary lending markets. Their direct purchases of bank debt has allowed for banks to make and sell more loans. This again has resulted in an increase in the supply of loanable funds.

As previously mentioned, the asset purchasing program also involved the Fed buying Treasuries. Keep the market for loanable funds in mind. The government is running massive deficits. Fiscal year 2009 deficit is expected to more than quadruple the record set in 2008. In other words, the demand side for loans has gone through the roof.

In a free market, this would result in higher interest rates, yet Treasuries are below the rate of inflation. Now, when you or I buy a U.S. Treasury note, we are lending money to the government. Naturally, if the rates are negative real, you, China, and I won't lend the government money. The Federal Reserve has stepped in and significantly contributed to the supply side. The term used to describe the Federal Reserve's purchases of mortgage and government debt is monetization. Monetization is when the Fed print dollars in order to buy debt.

Let's bring this whole thing full circle. The negative real federal funds rate and asset purchasing programs (1) allow for banks to borrow at negative real levels and write more loans, (2) increase demand in the secondary lending market, and (3) allow for the government to finance its debt at negative real levels.

Unfortunately, all of these policies are expansionary and therefore inflationary. If lenders incur losses when rates are negative real, who bites the bullet when the Fed is that lender? The answer is the value of the U.S. dollar. As the dollar declines, inflation rises, which means *interest rates have to rise*. As rates continue to experience more pressure, the Fed will have to increase its role in keeping them down. That will just result in more downward pressure on the dollar.

It's a snowball effect. That is why negative real rates set by the Fed have a finite timeline. The thing about price fixing, in any market, is that it can't be held off equilibrium forever. If the price is too cheap, like the price of money, demand will grossly outpace supply. If the price is too expensive, there will be a supply glut. I said that the lending market is not a free market, and it isn't. Imagine what the rates would be if the Fed was not conducting current policies.

A time will come when interest rates reflect real market conditions. Remember that the fair-value equations are affected by interest rates. More specifically, higher interest rates will give a higher premium to the futures price. All present-value calculations have grossly diverged from equilibrium. There will be a period in the not-so-distant future when these imbalances can be taken advantage of. Few will win, while many will lose. The potential profits to be had will be bountiful. Make sure you're on the right team.

Conclusion

In this chapter, we took a look at single stock futures and the benefits they present. The opportunities available from such an investment vehicle range from simple diversification to more extensive hedging techniques. The potential to secure profits and limit exposure to risk is spawned within the failure of theoretical valuation to represent actual market conditions. This set of circumstances is unique to the current economic climate and its associated volatility.

Understanding this concept is especially important for a vehicle such as single stock futures, but it's relevant across the whole field of finance. The inability to recognize both the risk and the opportunity is equivalent to walking around "blind without a cane."

Notes

1. David G. Downey, "Single Stock Futures: An Alternative to Securities Lending," OneChicago, 2009. Available at www.onechicago.com/wp-content/uploads/content2009/single-stock-futures-an-alternative-to-securities-lending1.pdf. Also, Howard L. Simons, "Calculate the Savings with Single-Stock Futures," OneChicago, 2009. Available at www.onechicago.com/wp-content/uploads/content2009/calculate-the-savings-with-single-stock-futures.pdf.
2. The CPI figures are taken from the August report of the Bureau of Labor Statistics. All other figures are from Bloomberg.

CHAPTER

10

International Investing: China, India, and Other Emerging Markets

There is no doubt about it—a diversified investor must have exposure to the foreign emerging markets in order to have a well-rounded portfolio. Emerging markets provide U.S. investors a nice way to limit exposure to systemic risk.

This chapter will go over BRIC countries, as well as Eastern Europe, Africa, and Latin America. We will also provide information on how to invest in these markets. Remember that investing is at its most efficient when it is most businesslike. Never put all your eggs in one basket and remember to diversify.

International Investing: A Passport to Global Growth

With the boom of once-third-world countries like China and India, the world is moving closer and closer to a truly international economy. In this new economy, globalization and the breaking down of barriers have facilitated freer trade and more open markets, resulting in a complex and constantly evolving investment landscape.

The world may be getting smaller and more interconnected, but a globally diversified portfolio remains fundamental to a well-planned investment strategy. As the legendary pioneer of global investing Sir John Templeton once said, "Investors should see the investment world as an ocean and buy where you get the most value for your money."

Much like corporations that are becoming more geographically mobile to take advantage of lower costs, expanding markets, and more hospitable business environments, smart investors would be well served to expand their horizons across borders to capitalize on long-term growth opportunities in emerging markets and to diversify internationally to help reduce risk.

Even with the recent economic downturn that has battered global stocks and devastated emerging markets, there are still good reasons to invest overseas. It is clear that a new world order has dawned—one that U.S. markets and the West no longer dominate.

Although the United States is home to the world's largest financial marketplace, nearly two-thirds of the world's stock market capitalization lies beyond American borders. Many countries' economies continue to grow at a faster rate than the United States'. And over the long term, emerging markets have outperformed their developed-market counterparts, and that includes U.S. stocks.

For a snapshot of developing economies' potential, consider the numbers: China, India, Mexico, Brazil, and Russia have a combined population of approximately three billion people, nearly 10 times the U.S. population. However, their combined gross domestic product (GDP) is only half of the U.S. GDP. These countries haven't even begun to realize their true, fully efficient economic output. Of course, skeptics will say that there is a reason for such grossly disproportionate GDP levels between these countries and the United States—often citing noncapitalist governments as the driving force.

While that might be true, it doesn't negate the fact that these economies are growing, and growing quickly. Several of the aforementioned countries are experiencing terribly impressive annual growth rates: about 9.5 percent over the past 20 years in China and about 6 percent in India compared with less than 3 percent in the United States. (The Chinese and Indian economies are expected to continue to grow at 7 percent to 9 percent annually for the foreseeable future; the United States is expected to grow at 2.6 percent.)[1]

On average, these countries' industrial sectors account for 30 percent of their GDP, and as a whole, they plan to make several trillion dollars in infrastructure investments over the next several years. They are experiencing an industrial revolution similar to that of the United States in the early twentieth century, and unless there is some sort of apocalypse, these countries are going to continue to grow.

The so-called BRIC countries—Brazil, Russia, India, and China—are well on their way to dominating the world economy. As their economies grow and the populations become wealthier, there will be more demand for global products, thus significantly stimulating the world economy.

Don't take that statement the wrong way and think that I mean the American economy is doomed—because that is certainly not the case at all. American products and services will always be in high demand. It is no secret that America has left its industrial roots and has become a service industry of sorts, but with that, our largest export has become creation and innovation. We pioneered the Internet, the personal computer, the cell phone, and now the all-in-one iPhone—all of which have changed humankind forever.

Since America has moved away from the industrial powerhouse it once was, the American population has more time to spend pushing the creative industries like technology and entertainment to new levels. This allows America to dominate the global market of what is cool and what isn't. And as long as the world population is watching America's movies and listening to America's music on American web sites like Hulu and Apple's iTunes, all while talking on their iPhones, then the American economy will always have some sort to stake in the world economy. Now, if we could only pull our act together in regards to green technology.

Anyway, it is obvious that Europe and America can no longer just brush aside countries like China and India as nonthreats or third-world underlings. These countries are the front-runners in a long line of up-and-coming economies that want to plant a stake in the global money pie.

A World of Opportunity

Many investors are reluctant to invest internationally because they mistakenly believe the largest, most successful companies are located in the United States. The fact is that nearly two-thirds of Fortune Global 500 companies are based abroad, and 15 of the top 25 corporations on the list are headquartered in foreign countries, primarily Europe and Asia. Moreover, many American corporate success stories have a strong presence throughout the world; and a number of large foreign companies maintain significant operations within U.S. shores.

Emerging markets' burgeoning economies are creating ripe opportunities to take full advantage of growth industries that have long dried up on this side of the pond. And businesses with operations or strong partnerships in emerging economies often have international assets not directly linked to the negative financial realities at home.

The Safe Haven of Diversification

Diversification is about more than just gaining exposure to different asset classes, sectors, and company sizes. It's also about providing geographic diversification. Investing overseas reduces risk by insulating a portfolio against declines tied to the performance of a single economy that ravage some investors during the market's most difficult periods. With that in mind, investing in firms with broad global exposure not only hedges exposure to the volatility of the U.S. economy but also takes full advantage of currency fluctuations, foreign sales, and growth in overseas markets.

Currency Fluctuations

When investing internationally, the changing value of world currencies could significantly impact financial returns. These fluctuations sometimes work in investors' favor and at other times work against them. When the U.S. dollar gains against foreign currencies, holdings lose value because the foreign currency purchases fewer dollars. (A stronger American economy, higher U.S. interest rates, or a lower trade deficit could boost the dollar's value.) Conversely, when the dollar is weak and loses value against foreign currencies, the value of securities and assets denominated in other currencies is boosted, even if share prices stay flat.

For example, the dollar depreciated 36 percent between 2001 and 2008 against the euro, making investments denominated in the European currency worth 56 percent more once converted back to dollars—and that doesn't take into account any investment gains.

High Risk/Return

It's prudent to remember that many emerging markets are located in nations with histories of political and economic instability, which could subject their stocks to wide price swings. But the trade-off for a higher degree of risk is the possibility of greater long-term returns.

Emerging markets, which are home to 85 percent of the world's population, account for nearly half of the global GDP. Unlike the world's developed nations, whose economies are mature and financial markets well established, emerging markets have experienced or are on the verge of explosive economic and stock market growth.

Admittedly, the United States remains the undisputed global leader in overall corporate strength and individual prosperity. But other countries that have adopted the American brand of capitalism are also home to many of the world's most successful corporations and growing consumer classes.

That said, investments confined to the United States limit growth potential. Opening your investment portfolio's door to the world invites in opportunity and diversification, allowing you to gain exposure to different economies, industries, and stock markets, greatly enhancing return potential and limiting overall volatility.

Everything considered, international investing offers the potential for strong diversification, broader opportunities, and enhanced returns. Looking ahead, emerging markets hold more promise than ever before.

The geopolitical and global economic ramifications are undeniable.

Emerging-Market Opportunities

China

China has the third-largest economy in the world, after the United States and Japan, and its influence on the global economy continues to increase.

With a population of 1.3 billion and one of the emerging market's highest-octane economies, China has become a twenty-first-century powerhouse and a magnet for foreign capital. Since its entry into the World Trade Organization in 2001, China has doubled its share of global manufacturing output, fueling a stock market boom and helping it amass a $2 trillion stockpile of foreign currency reserves.[2]

Not long ago, the prospect of investing in China was intimidating. Skeptics doubted China would ever become a stable society with an open economy. China was a sleeping dragon, economically depressed and politically unyielding—a frightening place viewed with suspicion, pessimism, and trepidation. But investors who have embraced China know that to avoid the "Middle Kingdom" based upon old conceptions is to forgo one of the most exciting and promising opportunities in the world today.

Case in point: China has clocked economic growth each year since its free-market reforms of 1978. Its $2.8 trillion economy, leading the world in information technology and low-cost consumer exports, is growing at a rate of 9 percent a year on average—6 full points faster than the United States. China is the world's largest producer of cement, steel, aluminum, copper, and coal. It dominates the low-end consumer market in everything from clothing to consumer electronics, and if projections hold, China could surpass the United States as the world's largest economy in as little as 20 years.

It is easy to dismiss such breakneck growth as bubble-economy hubris—until you consider the reality on the ground. When China confidently stepped onto the world stage at the 2008 Summer Olympic Games in Beijing, the country seemed light-years away from the bleak days when armies of workers and civil servants in drab Communist garb rode bicycles to work in run-down factories and Mao Zedong–era brick-and-concrete buildings. Beijing and Shanghai have both grown and evolved at warp speed, becoming virtually unrecognizable. Shanghai has become a high-tech, skyscraper-filled international business hub and Beijing a world-class capital to rival any city in North America or Europe. Once-run-down factory districts now boast some of the world's largest industrial zones, with modern office towers and high-tech research and development (R&D) centers. Per capita income has tripled in a generation, propelling some 300 million out of poverty.[3]

Far more than merely a source of cheap goods and labor, China has also developed a huge domestic market, with a growing number of goods being produced for a rising middle class endowed with rising purchasing power and a thirst for Western-style-creature comforts. Much like fashionable Americans, upwardly mobile Chinese consumers view products as status symbols and are demanding the latest designer goods and cutting-edge technologies at a breakneck pace. In 2007, China's passenger car market became the third largest in the world. China has more cell phone users than anywhere, a number approaching 700 million. And it has overtaken the United States in total number of homes with broadband Internet connections.[4]

Perhaps the closest parallel to the emergence of China in the twenty-first century is the nineteenth-century Industrial Revolution in America. Fueled by the rise of the coal and iron era, with a massive economy stoked by entrepreneurial drive and hard work, the United States flourished to lead the world in agriculture, textile production, and period technology, such as the telegraph, electricity, and steam engines. China is now a country with an explosive economy and an educated, low-wage workforce that will ensure it dominates manufacturing and export markets for the foreseeable future.

Clearly, the United States and other established powers have made room for China, which has the weight and dynamism to transform the twenty-first-century global economy. China, in almost every economic sphere—production, exports of goods and services, investing, the use of energy and commodities, and consumer markets—is now a major player. As China's economy matures, its newly confident companies are flexing their muscles and showing global ambition.

For its part, the Chinese government has embarked on a monumental infrastructure build-out that is consuming half of the world's cement, 40 percent of its steel, and 20 percent of its copper. It has also made great strides in the areas of intellectual property rights, corporate governance, regulation, and transparency, making China much more attractive to foreign investment. Beijing, which aspires to make China a global incubator for innovation in technology, business, and finance, has a more open-minded, market-savvy, and probusiness leadership that is ambitiously laying the groundwork for decades of continued prosperity.

For growth-oriented investors seeking new opportunities, there is a compelling case for investing in China.

India

India is without question waking to global economic power. The subcontinent is home to more than a billion people, and the Indian economy is today the twelfth-largest in the world and the second-fastest growing major economy after China—a perpetual work in progress with an increasingly diversified mix of services, agriculture, and manufacturing.

India's GDP is on track to reach the $2 trillion mark by 2015, driven by an advantageous combination of favorable demographics, economic reforms, and the rolling tide of globalization. Barring catastrophe, within 30 years, India will overtake Germany as the world's third-biggest economy.[5]

Although the global economic meltdown has caused a considerable decline in foreign investment, taking a huge toll on virtually every domestic sector and slowing its growth rate, India remains one of the most promising developing nations.

For starters, the country is the world's top outsourcing hub, specializing in information technology (IT) technical support, software engineering, and call center operations. The list of companies that outsource to India reads like a veritable Who's Who of International Business, including: IBM, Microsoft, Intel, Dell, Oracle, Cisco, Hewlett-Packard, FedEx, UPS, Boeing, Prudential, GE Capital, TransUnion, EDS, Qwest, Rand McNally, and even Wal-Mart.

But it's emerging as more than an outsourcing-services destination. Agriculture is big business in India, which ranks second in the world in farm output. Agriculture and related sectors like forestry, logging, and fishing employ approximately 60 percent of the nationwide workforce. India is the world's leading producer of tea, milk, black pepper, bananas, cashews, ginger, coconuts, and turmeric; it is the second-largest producer of sugar, wheat, rice, and inland fish and has the world's largest cattle population. Despite a steady decline of its share in the GDP, agriculture is still the country's largest economic sector, playing a crucial role in its development.

The South Asian nation has more going for it than its old mainstay. Its manufacturing machine is also picking up speed. Although industrial production only accounts for a fifth of India's economic output as compared with two-fifths of China's, this ratio is rising fast. Its number of exports to the United States is rising faster percentagewise than China's, albeit on a much smaller scale. Annual growth in manufacturing output today stands at 9 percent—just behind services growth, which is growing at a rate of 10 percent.[6]

Taking advantage of a fast-growing, young, tech-savvy, and English-speaking talent pool, companies like General Motors, Motorola, John Deere, LG Electronics of South Korea, and the Netherlands' Mittal Steel have built factories in India to manufacture products for domestic sale and export to the U.S. and European markets.

For all the momentum it now enjoys, India does face certain challenges as a burgeoning economic powerhouse. Infrastructure, the backbone of a modern economy, is severely lacking, leaving India playing catch-up to bring its antiquated roads, electrical grid, and ports up to snuff. Electricity blackouts and chronic power shortages are common throughout the country (particularly in the north), and dirt roads still exist, even in cities like Bangalore, India's Silicon Valley—a hotbed of technological innovation. Ports are straining under the weight of rising exports. And the country's inadequate education system lacks the academic and research chops to support India's ambition of becoming a center for computer science and product R&D.

Despite these obstacles, there is a new optimism both in India and on Wall Street as the Asian elephant prepares for future growth.

Russia

Central Moscow paints a rosy picture of the state of Russia's economy. In its prestigious Ostozhenka neighborhood (called the "Golden Mile"), multimillion-dollar penthouses are home to the barons of industry. The streets are filled with luxury cars, gourmet restaurants, and upscale shops. Nearby, overlooking the Moskva River, gleaming steel and glass skyscrapers form the Moscow International Business Center, a $12 billion development destined to become the city's new financial heart.

But dig a bit deeper, and things aren't exactly what they seem. Since the fall of the Soviet Union in the early 1990s, Russia has struggled to transition from a centrally planned Socialist economy to a modern market-based one. Even as the Russian government continues its efforts to achieve consistent economic growth and become a first-world economy, it is still a place heavily influenced by petrodollars, nouveau riche tycoons, politics, and sometimes anarchy.

Organized crime, corruption, and political pressure have become ingrained in Russian business culture, with everyone from investigative journalists to corporate executives becoming targets of harassment, threats, extortion, physical assaults, and even assassination. The show trials of Yukos Oil Company founder Mikhail Khodorkovsky; the embarrassing fraud and theft scandal involving international investment fund Hermitage Capital, Russia's leading foreign investor; and retail giant Ikea's decision to suspend further investment in Russia because of pervasive demands for bribes haven't helped matters. President Dmitry Medvedev has called corruption and reform of Russia's legal system two of the most serious challenges facing the country.

The Council of Europe agrees. In a June 2008 report entitled "Allegations of Politically Motivated Abuses of the Criminal Justice System in Council of Europe Member States," the 47-nation body cited troubles including "pressure on judges," frequent "intimidation and reprisals" against defense and civil attorneys, "irregularities in the investigative process," and "political interference in the criminal justice process" as widespread. These findings will likely impact potential business partners' and investors' perceptions, negatively affecting Russia's business climate and economic development.

So, why bother investing in Russia at all? In a word: growth. Russia ended 2008 with its tenth straight year of growth, averaging 7 percent annually. And although economic and investment growth have slowed considerably, Prime Minister Vladimir Putin's government is moving to stimulate credit markets and revive the economy. Even with all its flaws—compounded by an economy hard-hit by the global financial crisis—Russia remains one of the fastest-growing economies in the world.[7]

It's also the world's largest energy seller, producing more natural gas than any other nation (about 25 percent of the global supply) and exporting more oil than anywhere, aside from Saudi Arabia (its Ural crude oil accounts for roughly 10 percent of the world's total production). Russia also has an expansive mining industry, with access to 26 percent of global iron ore reserves and 11 percent of the world's coal. It is also responsible for 20 percent of global nickel and cobalt production. When all is said and done, Russian stocks will likely rebound on commodity demand from China, India, and other developing nations.[8]

Economists at the Organization for Economic Cooperation and Development (OECD) predict robust future GDP growth, which will ultimately help launch Russia's economy into the modern age.

Eastern Europe

Twenty years after the fall of the Berlin Wall and collapse of the Iron Curtain, Eastern Europe has become the continent's most dynamic and promising region. The former Soviet bloc nations' free-market economies are growing fast. But problems persist across the region: crime and corruption, slow growth, and political turmoil stirred by those feeling a sense of post–Cold War insecurity.

Nevertheless, countless multinationals have embraced the East as the ideal place to establish low-cost manufacturing and other offshore operations—from drug, auto, and aerospace plants to corporate back offices—conveniently situated on Western Europe's doorstep. This led to Western and Asian companies pouring billions of dollars in foreign investment into places like Poland, Romania, the Czech Republic, Slovakia, Bulgaria, and Hungary, allowing them to play an increasingly important role in the global economy.

Like virtually everywhere else, Eastern Europe hasn't been immune to the impact of the global meltdown, which has weakened demand for commodities and exports and put a strain on regional credit markets.

Poland, the region's largest economic power and Europe's biggest coal producer, is holding up much better than most in the European Union (despite rising unemployment, the economy's worst slump in almost a decade), thanks in large part to Warsaw's sound economic policies. The government is aggressively focused on energy security and reducing greenhouse gas emissions, establishing deeper economic ties with Persian Gulf states like gas-rich Qatar, South Korea, with whom it's considering cooperating on building nuclear power plants and a liquefied natural gas terminal.

Romania has the region's second-largest economy, which in 2008 grew faster than any other in the European Union. But 2009 saw tightening credit slow private lending, reduce wage growth, and prompt manufacturers to cut output. Its economy has been further plagued by ballooning foreign debt, massive government spending, and a sharp reversal of market sentiment. Its saving grace is the fact that it boasts the region's largest gas fields and petrochemical industry.[9]

The Czech Republic's small, open economy has the highest GDP per capita in the region. Unfortunately, a sharp drop in foreign direct investment in 2009 along with sagging auto production, the backbone of Czech exports, has taken a toll on growth in the economy, which is heavily dependent on exports.

Despite major headwinds causing global demand for consumer goods to tumble and factory production and assembly activity to slide, the Czech Republic's strong manufacturing base's close ties to Western European markets will likely make for a relatively speedy recovery and offer substantial stock bargains once the global economy gets back on track.

In Eastern Europe, as anywhere, short-term risk and periodic bouts of volatility are to be expected, but by any reasonable measure, the long-term economic forecast is bright.

Latin America

Latin America was once plagued by political populism, poor fiscal management, rampant inflation, and volatile interest rates.

However, before the global nosedive, economies throughout much of the region had made complete turnarounds, gaining stability and showing brisk growth for several years. Rising demand from China for fossil fuels and metals helped fuel economic expansion and booming stock markets (trade between Latin America and China jumped from $10 billion in 2000 to $140 billion in 2008).[10]

The governments of Brazil and Mexico, the two largest Latin economies, have successfully instituted smart macroeconomic policies that have kept a lid on inflation and brought interest rates back to earth.

A result of the global economic shockwave, the region has felt the sting of the collapse in commodity prices, and its currencies have plunged. Mexico has seen its worst recession since the Tequila Crisis of 1995. A marked drop in trade has hurt exports (80 percent of which go to the United States), and access to credit, which not long ago fueled a boom in consumer spending, has all but dried up.

Brazil continues to attract foreign venture capital during the economic storm, even with its high taxes and restrictive labor laws. The South American nation, which has one of the fastest-growing emerging economies in the world, has an expanding domestic marketplace marked by a healthy appetite for clothing, personal computers, cell phones, real estate, and automobiles (car sales have risen 80 percent since 2005). This market, along with oil and agricultural product exports and sales of high-grade iron ore to steelmakers around the world, is already helping Brazil's economy to bounce back.

The Portuguese-speaking nation has a healthy banking system, investment-grade national debt, and relatively diverse trade ties that help insulate it from the ravages of the global economic pullback. The commodity-producing nation has also turned what was once a hefty trade deficit into a large surplus ($207 billion in foreign reserves), strengthening its currency, reducing its debt load, lowering interest rates, and opening credit markets to individuals and businesses.

All things considered, Brazil is likely to continue growing for many years to come, providing investors with opportunities to cash in on its strong commodity sector and evolving consumer economy.

Other Latin American countries are also fairing well.

Peru's export revenue has suffered due to declining metals prices, but the government is tapping three years of surpluses to fund a massive stimulus plan to offset a private investment glut. Increased spending in infrastructure will ensure continued economic growth in Peru, which has held up well in the face of the slump, being one of a handful of emerging markets to maintain growth. The year 2008 saw the launch of Peru's first exchange-traded fund, and the Lima Stock Exchange began listing global ETFs to meet growing investor demand for international exposure.

Colombia's export-driven economy has had a harder time of it, with exports taking huge blows on weaker demand. As the global economy picks up steam, oil, coffee, and coal (Colombia's three main exports) should lead the way during the recovery.

Although Argentina's economy ground to a halt for the first time in close to seven years in 2008 amid slumping industrial production and construction decline, exports will bounce back, allowing the country to continue growing and to add to its trade surplus. (Argentina is one of the world's largest exporters of beef and other agricultural goods, with food accounting for around one-third of its total exports.)

Chile produces more copper than any other nation, and the soft metal is the country's biggest export (salmon holds the number two spot); it is the leading exporter of fresh fruit in the Southern Hemisphere; and wine exports to the European Union and United States are growing with ramped-up production. (Chile is now the fifth-largest producer of wine in the world.)[11]

The nation's economic policies have helped offset the effects of the global recession. The Santiago Stock Exchange is working with issuers to bring exchange-traded funds to Chile as the government pushes for new regulations governing ETFs as part of an economic reform package aimed at increasing Chile's capital market activity and global competitiveness.

Waves of multinational corporations, institutional investors, venture capitalists, and individual players have strategically positioned themselves to capitalize on Latin America's phenomenal growth and the rapid spread of free-market capitalism.

Africa

For decades, Africa has been a languid, inhospitable investment backwater—with many of its 53 nations rived by civil war and dogged by poverty and political instability. This is where mineral wealth was stripped and exploited by multinational corporations and lives ravaged by puppet dictators installed by colonial powers. It has kept the United Nations, the International Monetary Fund, and the World Bank quite busy.

Today, although Africa is the poorest continent in the world and attracts the least investment, many of its countries are realizing growth. In recent years, interest in Africa by investors has surged, driven by its abundant commodity staples, increasing macroeconomic stability, and long-awaited political reforms bringing the promise of reduced corruption and strengthened governance.

Leading the way is South Africa. Once plagued by Apartheid, it now has sub-Saharan Africa's biggest and most stable economy, vast natural resources, a well-developed infrastructure, and one of the largest stock exchanges in the world.

South Africa hasn't been left unscathed by the global market turmoil. Its economy slipped into recession in 2008 for the first time since 1992, as softening local and global demand left its traditionally strong mining and manufacturing sectors scaling back output and slashing workforces. The government has responded by severely cutting interest rates to ease pressure on the economy. It has also targeted reducing unemployment; improving its health care, education, and justice systems; and increasing infrastructure spending. Officials project South Africa's economy to grow 2.5 to 3.5 percent annually for several years after the recovery.[12]

Nigeria, Africa's second-most populous nation and its leading oil producer, has an economy almost totally reliant on crude exports.

Unfortunately, weaker energy prices and lower oil output coupled with pipeline attacks by armed militant groups—who have sabotaged pumping stations, blown up pipelines, and abducted foreign oil workers—have wrecked havoc on the country's petroleum industry and thus Nigeria's economy. The boom that enabled Nigeria to realize record annual growth since 1999 is over. Making peace with rebel factions and further development and diversification of its economy will be vital for Nigeria to bounce back when the recession ends.

Ghana, one of Africa's most stable and prosperous democracies, is the world's second-largest cocoa exporter (after their neighbor the Ivory Coast) and Africa's number two gold producer (after South Africa). The West African nation has been grappled with a deep budget deficit and large trade imbalance since fuel and food import costs reached record highs in 2007. The recent discovery of oil offshore will add a new revenue stream to Ghana that has the potential to be a catalyst to improve its creditworthiness and lure new investment.

Since the end of its bloody civil war in 2002, Angola has vastly increased oil production, pumping somewhere between 1.5 million and 2 million barrels of oil a day, more than any other African nation aside from Nigeria. Once awash in cash with an economy that grew a mind-boggling 24 percent in one year, lower crude prices and quotas imposed by the Organization of Petroleum Exporting Countries (OPEC) have hit Angola hard where it hurts. Oil is vital to Angola's economic development, as it is responsible for more than 90 percent of the country's income.[13]

Kenya, which has East Africa's biggest economy, depends heavily on tourism, agriculture, and textiles. Though it has been on the road to economic recovery since 2003, postelection violence in early 2007 slowed tourism, stifled farm production, and rattled investors. Since then, growth and infrastructure development has been dragged down by political wrangling, drought, energy shortages, and a lack of financial capital. Even so, Kenya's economy is expected to continue expanding.[14]

The so-called Dark Continent faces immense challenges including widespread political uncertainty, staggering foreign debt, poor infrastructure, and inadequate foreign direct investment. But all things taken into account, it has nowhere to go but forward.

African consumers are eager for a slice of the good life, or at least a better life, and investment opportunities abound, ranging from commodities to construction and financial services to retail.

Largely untapped Africa has the potential, in time, to become the next big thing.

How and Where to Trade in Emerging Markets

Today, playing international markets is easier than ever before, with several options for every type of investor.

Mutual Funds

Mutual funds pool money from hundreds or thousands of investors to build a portfolio of stocks, bonds, real estate, or other securities, providing each of the fund's investors with a slice of the pie while making diversification easy and requiring only modest minimum investments.

Most mutual fund companies offer funds for investing in international markets, the most basic of which are international and global funds. International funds invest solely outside of North America, while global funds invest worldwide, including North America (many, as much as 50 percent in the United States, limited foreign exposure). There are also regional and country-specific funds.

There are risks associated with all investments, but emerging-market mutual funds have particular pitfalls to consider that can negatively impact your investment:

Taxes: If mutual funds managers redeem positions late in the year to lock in capital gains, these "embedded capital gains" are distributed to shareholders on a pro rata basis.

Risk: Investing in funds weighted toward developing nations bring volatility inherent with immature economies.

Expenses: Specialty overseas funds with a single country or regional focus often carry higher fees than domestic funds. (Those without active management strategies are less expensive options.)

Currency: Waxing and waning foreign currency values compared with the U.S. dollar can heavily affect short-term performance.

Benchmarks: Locating a benchmark to act as a gauge for measuring a fund's performance against rivals can be next to impossible with emerging-market funds.

Here is a list of four top-performing funds over the past five years:

> DFA Emerging Markets Value I (DFEVX)
>
> Oppenheimer Developing Markets Y (ODVYX)
>
> Evergreen Emerging Markets Growth I (EMGYX)
>
> Lazard Emerging Markets Equity Institutional (LZEMX)

Exchange-Traded Funds

Gone are the days when the world's stock exchanges were clubby nonprofits, mere vehicles for traders, brokers, and individual investors to swap stocks, securities, commodities, and derivatives. In an increasingly competitive world, today's exchanges are investments in their own right.

With that in mind, exchange-traded funds are increasingly popular alternatives to mutual funds for tapping the growth of emerging markets. Long used by traders and savvy investors, ETFs have gained favor with individual investors in recent years.

In their international form, these financial vehicles—essentially investment companies with shares that trade on stock exchanges in foreign markets—allow investors to buy shares (through a broker or in a brokerage account) that trade like the stock of any publicly traded security but track indexes such as the Bombay Stock Exchange or closely watched sectors like Argentina's commodity stocks. Like mutual funds, they have the benefit of being diversified against undue risk. However, unlike actively managed mutual funds, most have more affordable fees and tend to offer returns in line with their benchmarks. They also provide active investors with the ability to more nimbly move in and out of foreign markets at a lower cost. (While some ETFs have high expenses, they are almost always lower than comparable mutual funds.)

There are generally two ways for international investors to use ETFs. The first is a broader-based way involving investing in regional ETFs (Eastern Europe, the Far East, Latin America, etc.). The second way is to buy ETFs that represent specific countries like China, India, or Brazil. Both approaches allow you to tailor your investments to your own preferences, strategies, and goals.

The Tax Advantages of ETFs   Because ETFs track indexes that usually buy and sell securities far less frequently than their mutual fund counterparts (trades generally occur in the secondary market without involving the fund itself), most ETFs rarely bring with them end-of-the-year capital gains distributions; iShares, the largest family of ETFs, has never distributed any capital gains to its investors. In contrast to mutual fund investors, ETF shareholders buy and sell on an exchange, so transactions do not affect other shareholders, providing for more control and tax transparency.

Exchange-traded funds can also allow you to reduce your tax burden. For example, if you own a mutual fund that has declined since its purchase and you want to apply the capital loss while still maintaining market exposure, you could sell the mutual fund and simultaneously invest the proceeds in a similar ETF, thereby conducting a tax swap. Using this wash-sale rule is as simple as purchasing a security that is related but not identical within 30 days after a sale, effectively deferring the capital loss and lowering your overall tax liabilities.

Notes

Popular emerging-market ETFs include the following:

Total

> iShares MSCI Emerging Markets Index Fund (EEM)
>
> PowerShares FTSE RAFI Emerging Markets Portfolio (PXH)
>
> Vanguard Emerging Markets ETF (VWO)
>
> SPDR S&P Emerging Markets ETF (GMM)

Multiregion

> Claymore/BNY BRIC (Brazil, Russia, India, China) ETF (EEB)
>
> iShares MSCI BRIC Index Fund (BKF)
>
> BLDRS Emerging MKTS 50 ADR Index Fund (ADRE)
>
> streetTRACKS SPDR S&P BRIC (Brazil, Russia, India, China) 40 ETF (BIK)

Asia

> iShares FTSE/Xinhua China 25 Index (FXI)
>
> PowerShares Golden Dragon Halter USX China (PGJ)

SPDR S&P China (GXC)

First Trust ISE Chindia (China and India) ETF (FNI)

PowerShares India (PIN)

WisdomTree India Earnings (EPI)

Latin America

iShares S&P Latin America 40 Index Fund (ILF)

SPDR S&P Emerging Latin America ETF (GML)

Eastern Europe

SPDR S&P Emerging Europe ETF (GUR)

Africa

SPDR S&P Emerging Middle East and Africa ETF (GAF)

Invesco PowerShares MENA Frontier Countries Portfolio (PMNA)

International ADRs

First introduced to the investment world by J.P. Morgan, American depository receipts, called ADRs for short, offer a way to invest overseas inexpensively. Through them, investors can acquire stock in companies around the globe without having to purchase shares directly on foreign exchanges.

The concept behind ADRs is simple. Usually, a U.S. financial institution or investment firm will place a foreign company's stock in its vault, hence the name "depository." Issues held are priced in U.S. dollars, and investors may buy shares found in the collection by trading them on the market, just as if the company itself were selling them. One of the biggest benefits of using ADRs is the elimination of cross-border fees and the hassles that come with them.

American depository receipts investing generally generates some nominal fees, usually only amounting to a few pennies a year per ADR. And there are also several different types of ADRs, each with its own reporting requirements. Level I is the lowest, with the least stringent rules, trading over-the-counter (OTC). Level II and III ADRs are listed on the New York Stock Exchange, the American Stock Exchange, and the NASDAQ.

One thing you should be aware of before investing is that although the price of ADRs and underlying foreign shares are essentially equal, a single ADR share may not represent a single underlying at a one-to-one ratio. Ratios can vary from a fraction of a foreign share per ADR share to several thousand foreign shares per ADR share. For example, say a U.S. bank purchases 15 million shares from Chinese Toymaker Corporation and issues them at a ratio of 5:1. This means each ADR share you purchase is worth five shares on the Shanghai Stock Exchange. Be sure to have a clear understanding of what you're buying.

Most ADRs can be purchased through your regular brokerage or online trading account. But be aware that they carry additional risks because they are tied not only to a company's performance but also to local rates of inflation, currency values, and a country's economic and political environment.

Examples of Popular ADRs

3SBio (SSRX), a China-based biopharmaceutical company

Gushan Environmental Energy (GU), a Chinese biofuel producer

Baidu (BIDU), a Chinese Internet search engine

Infosys Technologies (INFY), an Indian outsourcer

Petroleo Brasileiro (PBR), a Brazilian oil producer

Anglogold Ltd. (AU), a South African gold miner

America Movil (AMX), a Mexican wireless telephone company

Taiwan Semiconductor (TSM), a Taiwanese semiconductor maker

Foreign Shares

It goes without saying that investing in individual stocks is best left to sophisticated investors with a keen nose for evaluating management teams, balance sheets, and the nuts and bolts of what makes a particular company a good play. This approach requires an ability to sniff out things like exceptional cash flows, positive earnings, high returns on invested capital, good profit margins, manageable or no debt, and growth prospects.

Many companies registered and headquartered abroad are listed on U.S. stock exchanges. Those that aren't can be purchased directly on global exchanges and are referred to as foreign ordinaries. These ordinaries can be traded in two ways: on the local exchange itself or though an American brokerage firm. Trades placed directly will occur when the market in question opens. Buys made through brokerages are usually transacted during U.S. market trading hours and sometimes incur fees for being traded when local markets are closed. Other fees can include the cost of accessing the foreign market, currency conversion fees, a custody fee for a local institution holding the shares, and costs associated with expediting trades.

For more information, see the following web sites:

- The web site www.morningstar.com offers comprehensive stock, mutual fund, and ETF research and analysis.
- The web site www.ADR.com is a valuable specialized resource to investors for conducting ADR research.
- At www.marketwatch.com/markets/emerging-markets, Dow Jones' MarketWatch provides constantly updated news on emerging markets.

For table purposes:

List of Top 25 Companies in the World (Fortune Global 500):

1. Wal-Mart Stores: United States
2. Exxon Mobil: United States
3. Royal Dutch Shell: the Netherlands
4. BP: Britain
5. Toyota Motors: Japan
6. Chevron: United States
7. ING Group: the Netherlands
8. Total: France
9. General Motors: United States
10. ConocoPhillips: United States
11. Daimler: Germany
12. General Electric: United States
13. Ford Motors: United States
14. Fortis: Belgium/the Netherlands
15. AXA: France
16. Sinopec: China

17. Citigroup: United States
18. Volkswagen: Germany
19. Dexia Group: Belgium
20. HSBC Holdings: Britain
21. BNP Paribas: France
22. Allianz: Germany
23. Crédit Agricole: France
24. State Grid: China
25. China National Petroleum: China

Conclusion

In this chapter, we covered international investing and how it is key in terms of diversification. We talked about the pros and cons of investing in countries like Russia and China, and we also went into detail on some of the more unknown markets like Africa and Latin America.

While actually investing in foreign stock might sound scary, there is a plethora of EFTs and managed products today that provide sound exposure to economies overseas.

This marks the last chapter of *The Profit Hunter*, and I hope this book helped shed some light on issues that both help and hurt the average investor. I want you to exploit the strategies outlined within to help you become a more successful investor and eventually achieve financial freedom.

Some parts of this book—especially the beginning—touch on some scary points: corruption on Wall Street, false financial fiduciaries, and unchecked gross government misspending of taxpayers' money. I don't want to be the bearer of bad news, but the fact is that these issues plague our freedom as United States citizens. Things like TARP and the Patriot Act (while intended to do good, have been abused) take our liberty away from us.

Freedom is a luxury that many Americans take for granted. I'm not sure of all the answers—but I do know when the fundamentals are off. That's one of the reasons I've had success in the market.

As Ben Franklin once said, "Any society that would give up a little liberty to gain a little security will deserve neither and lose both."

Notes

1. World Economic Forum, "China and the World: Scenarios to 2025," Executive Summary, 2008. Available at www.weforum.org/pdf/scenarios/china_executive_summary.pdf.

2. The People's Bank of China web site, 2009. Available at www.pbc.gov.cn/english/.
3. World Food Program press release, 2008. Available at www.wpf.org.
4. Xinhua News Agency, "China's Cell Phone Users Top 670 Million after 3G Services Start," 2009. Available at http://news.xinhuanet.com/english/2009-05/18/content_11397569.htm.
5. United Nations, "World Economic Situation and Prospects 2009." Available at www.un.org/esa/policy/wess/wesp2009files/wesp2009.pdf.
6. Indian Ministry of Commerce and Industry, 2009.
7. Central Intelligence Agency, *The World FactBook* (Washington, DC: Government Printing Office, 2009). Available at www.cia.gov/library/publications/the-world-factbook/index.html.
8. Keith Campbell, "Russian Mining Industry Showing Some Signs of Recovery," *Mining Weekly Online*, July 17, 2009.
9. KM Trust and Partners, Bucharest, Romania, 2009.
10. Zhou Xiaochuan, governor of China's central bank, at the Inter-American Development Bank's annual meeting in Medellin, Colombia, 2009.
11. Wines of Chile, Santiago web site, 2009. Available at www.winesofchile.org/.
12. Pravin Gorham, South Africa's finance minister, in his speech to Parliament, July 1, 2009.
13. Ricardo Gazel, "Angola: Perspectives on the Financial Crisis," World Bank, December 11, 2008. Available at http://blogs.worldbank.org/africacan/angola-perspectives-on-the-financial-crisis.
14. International Monetary Fund, Annual Article IV consultations assessment report, October 2008.

About the Author

Neil DeFalco has participated in almost every aspect of the capital and money markets. He is an expert in fundamental stock and option investing and carries with him a unique understanding of the global markets and economies. He studied Financial Economics at the University of Maryland and soon after began his career in the trenches of the Wealth Management Division at UBS Paine Webber. After gaining all of his licenses he moved on as a money manager for Morgan Stanley and then as an analyst for Ventura Investments. After several successful years he decided to start Oakshire Financial in order to help others achieve success in the stock market. DeFalco is a respected voice in the investment community and has been quoted on several prominent financial web sites, such as CNBC and MSN Money.

Index